ACTION PLAN
for IELTS

▶ *Last-minute preparation*

▶ *Practice test*

▶ *Self-study guide*

Vanessa Jakeman
Clare McDowell

CAMBRIDGE
UNIVERSITY PRESS

CAMBRIDGE
UNIVERSITY PRESS

University Printing House, Cambridge CB2 8BS, United Kingdom

Cambridge University Press is part of the University of Cambridge.

It furthers the University's mission by disseminating knowledge in the pursuit of education, learning and research at the highest international levels of excellence.

www.cambridge.org
Information on this title: www.cambridge.org/9780521615303

© Cambridge University Press 2006

First published 2006
12th printing 2014

Printed in Poland by Opolgraf

A catalogue record for this publication is available from the British Library

ISBN 978-0-521-61530-3 Self-study Student's Book (Academic module)
ISBN 978-0-521-61531-0 Self-study Student's Book (General Training module)
ISBN 978-0-521-61527-3 Self-study Pack (Academic module)
ISBN 978-0-521-61528-0 Self-study Pack (General Training module)
ISBN 978-0-521-61532-7 Cassette (for both modules)
ISBN 978-0-521-61533-4 CD (audio) (for both modules)

Designed and produced by HL Studios, Long Hanborough

Contents

Introduction

Who is *Action Plan for IELTS* for?

Action Plan for IELTS is a short, self-study guide for IELTS, containing one complete practice test. It is designed for students with a limited amount of time to prepare for the IELTS test or for students who have already completed an IELTS course and would like a last-minute guide to the test.

It is for students at intermediate level or above, and is designed for self-study, although it may also be used in class as part of a short preparation course. It shows students what skills are tested in IELTS, what type of questions and tasks they will see, and how to approach them.

There are two editions: one for the Academic module and one for the General Training module. Students should use the appropriate edition for their needs.

How is *Action Plan for IELTS* organised?

Action Plan for IELTS is organised by module: Listening, Reading, Writing and Speaking. These are presented in the same order as the actual test. Each of the four modules begins with a clear introduction, which gives full details of what to expect in that part of the test and what is tested. There is also an overview of the different question types for Listening and Reading, and an explanation of the marking criteria for Writing and Speaking.

Each part of each module gives examples of the Listening and Reading question types, and the Writing and Speaking tasks. The Writing section of the book is organised according to the marking criteria for this module. The criteria are illustrated with short exercises, so students can see exactly what the examiner is looking for and decide how best to approach these parts of the test. The Speaking section of the book provides a step-by-step guide to the three parts of the Speaking test.

The question types and tasks are accompanied by a short, effective *Action Plan*, which gives advice on ways to approach them, and suggests strategies to prepare students for the test. The *Key* includes answers to all the exercises, sample answers to the Writing tasks and, where appropriate, offers tips and strategies that can be used to help get the right answers. An *Audio CD/Cassette* accompanies all listening tasks, and the *Recording Scripts* are also provided.

At the end of the book, there is a complete IELTS *Practice Test*.

How can *Action Plan for IELTS* be used?

Action Plan for IELTS is flexible, and can be used in different ways:
- Students who don't know very much about the test and need a thorough overview should work systematically through the book, and then do the timed Practice Test at the end.
- Students who need more practice in one particular module may prefer to work through the book by doing all the Listening sections first, for example, followed by the Listening sections of the Practice Test, and so on.
- Students who are unsure about particular question types or tasks for the Listening and Reading sections can use the overview with the page references in the introduction for each skill and go directly to that section.

The Listening Test

A 30-minute test of your understanding of spoken English

How many sections does the listening test have?
There are four sections in the listening test. Each section has 10 questions, making a total of 40 questions. The sections become progressively harder. The answers to the questions come in the same order as the information on the recording.

Section 1 (3–4 minutes)
A conversation between two speakers on an everyday, social topic.

Section 2 (3–4 minutes)
A talk by one speaker on a general topic.

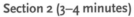

Section 3 (3–4 minutes)
A discussion between two to four speakers on a topic related to education.

Section 4 (3–4 minutes)
A lecture or talk by one speaker on an academic or study-related topic.

The whole test lasts about 30 minutes, including the instructions, your reading and listening time, and the time allowed for transferring your answers from the question paper to an answer sheet. The instructions are included on the recording.

- The listening test is the first part of the IELTS test.

- Arrive at the test room in plenty of time.

- Take a pencil and rubber with you.

- You write your answers on the question paper as you listen. You can use abbreviations at this stage if you want to.

- You have to transfer your answers to an answer sheet after the test. The recording gives you time to do this.

- You cannot take any books into the test room.

What is the listening test like?

A CD player or overhead sound system is used to play the test. Once the recording has started, you cannot enter or leave the room, or stop or interrupt the test.

There may be a lot of people in the room, so be prepared for this.

You hear the IELTS listening recording only ONCE, so you need to keep up with the questions and make good use of the words on the question paper to help you do this.

Where do I write my final answers?
You transfer your answers carefully from the question paper to an answer sheet at the end of the test.

Will I hear different accents?

Yes, but they will always be clear and easy to understand. You will not hear any grammatical mistakes.

What sort of questions will I get?

There are different question types in the listening test (see pages 8 and 9) and *you can get any mix of question types in any section of the test.* Often you have to choose the correct letter or write up to three words.

Will I get every question type in the test?

No. Each section of the test usually contains two or three question types, so in one complete listening test you could get a maximum of 12 different question types (usually you will get about eight or nine). Sometimes the same question type occurs in more than one section of the test. Remember, you may get a mix of the listening question types in any section of the test.

Why are there different listening situations and question types?

IELTS tests a range of listening skills that you need to live, work or study in an English-speaking environment. This means that you need to be able to understand different types of spoken English in a range of formal and informal contexts.

How can I make best use of the reading time?

You get time to read the questions in each section before you listen. Use this time to work out the topic, underline or highlight key words and decide what sort of information and answers you need to listen for.

What are key words?

Key words carry a lot of information. They are usually words such as nouns or verbs that help you understand the questions.

What general approach should I take to the listening test?

Once the recording begins, use the words on the question paper to help you keep your place. There is an example at the start of the test and the first three sections are divided into two parts to help you follow the conversation, discussion or talk. Write your answers on the question paper as you listen.

How can I improve my score in the listening test?

You can help to improve your score by making sure that you know what each question type tests and by having a general approach for each set of questions. The following pages, divided into four sections, provide you with an Action Plan for each set of questions.

What else can I do to prepare for the listening test?

You should listen to spoken English as often as possible, e.g. English-language radio, TV and other forms of media – even music.

How is the listening test marked?

There is one mark per question and this makes a total of 40 marks. Your mark is converted into a Band Score of between 1 and 9. You can get half bands in the listening test, e.g. 6.5.

Is correct spelling important?

Spelling should be correct and handwriting must be clear. Both British and American spellings are acceptable, e.g. *programme/program, colour/color,* but you should not use abbreviations. Numbers can be written as words or figures.

Overview of the Listening Question Types

Question type	Action	Key points	Page
Pick from a list	You pick the correct answers from a list of options.	• Write only the correct letters A, B, C, etc. • Answers may be worth one mark or more. • Answers can be written in any order.	10
Form filling	You complete the gaps in the form.	• Write up to three words and/or a number. • Check spelling.	12
Labelling a map or plan	You identify places on the map or plan.	• Write up to three words and/or a number. • If there is a box of answers to choose from, write the correct letter A, B, C, etc.	13
Sentence/ summary completion	You complete the gaps in the sentences or summary.	• Write up to three words and/or a number. • Check spelling. • Check grammar of sentence.	15
Table completion	You complete the table.	• Write up to three words and/or a number. • Check spelling.	17
Short answer questions	You answer the questions.	• Write up to three words and/or a number. • Answers may be worth one mark or more. • Check spelling.	18

Overview of the Listening Question Types

Question type	Action	Key points	Page
Multiple choice	You choose the correct letter A, B or C.	• Write only the correct letters A, B or C.	22
Matching	You match things together, e.g. places and people.	• Write only the correct letters A, B, C, etc. • Options may be used more than once.	23
Labelling a diagram	You label the parts on a diagram.	• Write up to three words and/or a number. • If there is a box of answers to choose from, write the correct letter A, B, C, etc.	24
Note completion	You complete the notes.	• Write up to three words and/or a number.	26
Flow chart completion	You complete the flow chart.	• Write up to three words and/or a number. • If there is a box of answers to choose from, write the correct letter A, B, C, etc.	28
Classification	You decide which category some words belong to.	• Write only the correct letters A, B, C, etc.	29

Listening Section 1

Section 1	Conversation (two speakers)	Social/survival	e.g. booking a hotel
Section 2	Talk by one speaker	General	e.g. radio talk
Section 3	Discussion (two to four speakers)	Educational	e.g. tutorial discussion
Section 4	Talk or lecture by one speaker	Course-related	e.g. university lecture

What is Section 1 like?
You will hear a conversation based on an everyday social/survival situation. Section 1 will help you get used to the listening exercises and test your understanding of simple facts, including names and numbers. There are always two speakers in Section 1. Here is an example of an extract from Section 1.

Hello. I'd like to book a table for four people for tomorrow night, please.

Certainly. Can I have your name and a contact phone number, please?

1 Tick the situations that you think belong to Section 1.

a	arranging to meet a friend	e	a discussion on the value of TV
b	a recorded talk at a museum	f	making a dental appointment
c	booking a holiday	g	a lecture on river pollution
d	negotiating an essay extension	h	ordering a product

Question Types and Practice Tasks

PICK FROM A LIST
You pick the correct answers from a list of options. There are usually two or three answers to pick from about six options. The options are labelled A, B, C, etc.

What does pick from a list test?
You have to pick out the correct facts from the recording and match these to words in the options. You may not hear the exact words that you read in the options, so you will be listening for a word or words with a similar meaning.

2 Match the words or phrases in Box A with words or phrases of a similar meaning in Box B.

A
> identification   study English
> fly   building   painting
> headgear   vehicle   meal
> bag   thunderstorm   winter spo
> rts

B
> helmet   suitcase   passport
> car   house   wet weather
> learn a language
> go by plane   lunch
> skiing   picture

How should I write my answers?

You only need to write the correct letters (A, B, C, etc.) on an answer sheet. You can write these in any order. Sometimes a question is worth one mark (for finding all the answers) and sometimes the question has one mark for each answer. This affects how you write your answers on the answer sheet.

ACTION PLAN

▶ Read the question carefully and note how many options you must pick.
▶ Underline or highlight the key words in the main question.
▶ Read the list of options and underline or highlight any key words.
▶ Re-phrase these options in your own words (if possible).
▶ As you listen, choose the correct answers.

NOW TRY THE TASK

Read the telephone conversation in the speech bubbles below and answer the questions.

Is that the Sydney Motor Registry? I'd like some information about taking a driving test. Do I need my own car, for instance?

Not necessarily. But first you must pass the knowledge test, that's the test of the road rules. That's done on a computer… here at this office. And you'll need to book for that. And then you can take the actual road driving test. That can be in your car or the driving school's car if you take lessons. And, of course, you must be at least 17 years old.

Questions 3–4

*Choose **TWO** letters A–E.*

● *Which **TWO** things must the girl do before she can take the road driving test?*

    A have her own car
    B have her own computer
    C pass the road rules test
    D book driving lessons
    E reach the age of 17

Note that this question is worth two marks because you have to understand quite a long conversation to get both answers.

FORM FILLING
You complete the gaps in the form using up to three words and/or a number. Some of the information may already be completed to help you.

What does form filling test?
Like all completion tasks, form filling tests your ability to predict what is missing in the gaps. You need to listen for important details like names, dates, places, times, etc. Sometimes these are spelt out. If they are not, you still need to try to spell the answers correctly. Make sure you can match spoken numbers to written numbers.

5 Say these times in two different ways, e.g. *two ten / ten past two in the afternoon.*

   2.10 pm   7.50 am   6.45 am   10.15 am   1.00 am   13.00 hrs

6 Say these dates in two different ways, e.g. *the first of February / February the first.*

   1st February 21st November 24 March December 22nd August 18

7 Look at the form below and decide what type of information you would need to

Casualty Department	Patient's admission details	Type of information
Family name	Mitchell	a name
Given name		a ....
Address	26 Lake Street, Newport	an address
Date of birth	....	b ....
Name of doctor	....	c ....
Reason for admission	....	d ....

listen for. Make a note in the column on the right.

How should I write my answers?
Write the correct words and/or numbers on the answer sheet. Use no more words than you are told to use and make sure you spell them correctly. You can write numbers in words or figures.

ACTION PLAN
▶ Read the instructions carefully to see how many words you can write.
▶ Look at the form and the information and decide what it is about.
▶ Note the order of the questions.
▶ Look at the gaps and any headings and decide what type of information is required.
▶ Underline or highlight the key words around each gap and use these to help you listen for the answer.
▶ As you listen, complete the form.

NOW TRY THE TASK

((((▶ Listen to Extract 1. (CD Track 1)

Questions 8–11

Complete the form below.
*Write **NO MORE THAN THREE WORDS AND/OR A NUMBER** for each answer.*

Motor Registry — Telephone messages

Caller's name	8 ....
Date of birth	9 ....
Telephone	10 *0412*......................
Type of car	11 ....

RECORDING SCRIPT PAGE 117

LABELLING A MAP OR PLAN
You identify places on the map or plan, using words and/or a number from a box of options. The parts to be labelled will have an arrow and the question number beside them.

Alternatively, places may already be identified on the map with letters. You match these letters to the information in the numbered questions.

What does labelling a map or plan test?
This type of question tests your ability to understand words and expressions of place and location. You must answer with information from the recording.

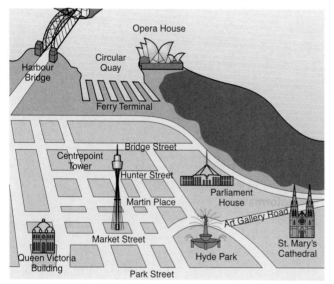

To practise using a map, look at the picture and answer the questions.

12 What is the building in the bottom left-hand corner?

13 Where on the map is St. Mary's Cathedral?

14 Name two streets that are parallel to Park Street.

15 What structure is at the top of the map in the middle?

How should I write my answers?
If you have a box of options, you only need to write the correct letter A, B, C, etc. Otherwise you write the words you hear on the recording. Only use the number of words you are told to use and remember to spell them correctly.

ACTION PLAN

▶ Look at the map or plan to form a general idea of the content.
▶ Look at the parts of the map or plan you need to label and decide what kinds of words are needed.
▶ Use the words already provided in the map or plan to guide your listening.
▶ When you listen, pay particular attention to expressions of location such as *in the middle, on the corner, next to, above/below, straight ahead,* **etc. as the** answer may depend on your understanding these words.
▶ As you listen, choose the correct answers.

NOW TRY THE TASK

(((▶ *Listen to Extract 2. (CD Track 2)*

Questions 16–19

Label the street plan below.
Write **NO MORE THAN THREE** *words for each answer.*

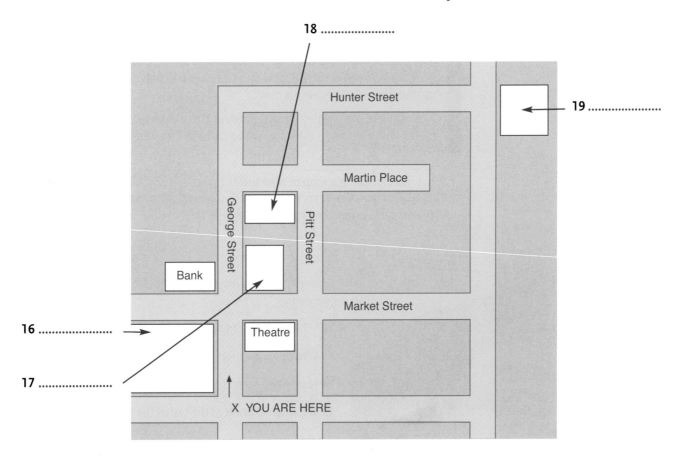

RECORDING SCRIPT PAGE 117
ANSWERS PAGE 108
⚷ PRACTICE TEST PAGE 92

Listening Section 2

Section 1	Conversation (two speakers)	Social/survival	e.g. booking a hotel
Section 2	**Talk by one speaker**	**General**	**e.g. radio talk**
Section 3	Discussion (two to four speakers)	Educational	e.g. tutorial discussion
Section 4	Talk or lecture by one speaker	Course-related	e.g. university lecture

These are the Question Types you will practise here
SENTENCE/SUMMARY
   COMPLETION
TABLE COMPLETION
SHORT ANSWER QUESTIONS

What is Section 2 like?
You will hear a talk by one speaker on a topic of general interest. Section 2 is a little harder than Section 1. You will have to decide what the important details or facts on the recording are, without the help of another speaker's questions to guide you.

1 Read these short talks. Decide where or when you might hear them. Pick out the important details in each one and complete the box below.

A *Welcome to Brighton Pavilion. You can pause this commentary at any time by pressing the red pause button. The Pavilion was initially built in 1784 and then re-built between 1815 and 1820 for the Prince Regent, who loved travelling. To celebrate this, he chose a mix of Indian and Chinese architectural styles for his palace, as you can see as you walk around.*

B *Koala bears are one of the most popular animals with visitors to our zoo because of their loveable appearance. However, a word of caution! They aren't always as nice as they look and they will happily use their long claws to protect themselves if they fear attack. So do take care.*

> **A** *Recorded audio tour /* ....
>
> **B** ....

Question Types and Practice Tasks

▶▶▶▶▶▶▶▶▶▶▶▶▶▶▶▶▶▶▶

SENTENCE/SUMMARY COMPLETION
You complete the sentences or summary by writing up to three words and/or a number in the gaps. The gaps can come at the beginning, in the middle or at the end of the sentence.

What is the difference between sentence and summary completion?
In the listening test, there is very little difference. Sentences are joined together to form a summary. Follow the **Action Plan** for sentence completion, remembering that sentences always have a main verb and a subject, and articles and prepositions are important and can be a useful guide to missing words.

2 Decide what type of information is needed to complete the sentences below. Is it a word, e.g. a noun, an adjective, a verb? Is it a number, e.g. a time, a measurement, an age?

Type of word(s)

Lectures begin at .... in the morning.   *a number (time)*

a *noun* can carry up to 350 passengers.
b *animal* are in danger of becoming extinct.
c The Rosetta Stone was discovered in Egypt in *date* .
d The tower is made of *something*
e Aboriginal art is extremely *adj.* these days.
f Research shows that cigarette smoking is *adj.* .

How should I write my answers?
If you have a box of options, you only need to write the correct answer A, B, C, etc. Otherwise you write the words you hear on the recording. Use no more words than you are told to use and make sure you spell them correctly. You can write numbers in words or figures.

ACTION PLAN

▶ Read the instructions carefully to see how many words you can write in your answer.
▶ Underline or highlight the key words in each question.
▶ Note the position of the gaps in the sentences.
▶ Decide what kind of information is needed to complete the sentences, e.g. a noun, a number, a verb or an adjective.
▶ Note any grammatical words in the questions, such as articles or prepositions, which can help you get the correct answer.
▶ Underline or highlight the key words around each gap and use these to listen for the answer.
▶ As you listen, complete the sentences or summary.

NOW TRY THE TASK

((◀ *Listen to Extract 1. (CD Track 3)*

Questions 3–6

Complete the sentences below.
*Write **NO MORE THAN THREE WORDS AND/OR A NUMBER** for each answer.*

3 The Bell Rock lighthouse was built almost *....200........* ago.
4 The tower is made of *...stone........* .
5 The reef is dangerous to ships because it is *under the water*
6 Initial construction took place during the *...summer......* .

7 How did you write the answer to question 3?

RECORDING SCRIPT PAGE 117

TABLE COMPLETION

You complete the table by writing up to three words and/or a number in the gaps provided. Some of the information may already be completed to help you.

How does table completion differ from sentence/summary completion?
In table completion you only have to fill in the gaps in the columns. There are no complete sentences.

8 Look at the table below. What is it about? What are the key words?
9 What kind of information is missing for hotels A, B and C?

	Rate per night	Rate includes	Hotel facilities
Hotel A	$75		TV in room
Hotel B			Swimming pool
Hotel C	$220	Full breakfast	

How should I write my answers?
Write the correct words and/or numbers on the answer sheet. Use no more words than you are told to use and make sure you spell them correctly. You can write numbers in words or figures.

ACTION PLAN

▶ Read the instructions carefully to see how many words you can write in your answer.
▶ Look at the table and the information included and decide what it is about.
▶ Look at the gaps and headings and decide what type of information is required.
▶ Note the order of the questions.
▶ Underline or highlight the key words around each gap and use these to listen for the answer.
▶ As you listen, complete the table.

NOW TRY THE TASK

((◀▶ Listen to Extract 2. (CD Track 4)

Questions 10–12

Complete the table below.
Write **NO MORE THAN THREE WORDS AND/OR A NUMBER** *for each answer.*

Cinema	Film	Times showing	Type of film
One	*Shrek 2*	**10**	animation
Two	**11**	6.15 pm	documentary
Three	*Armour of God*	5.30 / 9.15 pm	**12** ....

RECORDING SCRIPT PAGE 117

SHORT ANSWER QUESTIONS
You answer the questions using up to three words and/or a number.

What is involved in short answer questions?
There are two types of short answer question. Type 1 is where you answer an actual question, and Type 2 is where you make a list of up to three things. You need to underline or highlight the key words in the question that tell you what kind of information to listen out for. *Wh-* question words are often key words in Type 1 questions.

Where? *place*   **Which?** *thing*   **When?** *time*   **What?** *thing*
Why? *reason*   **Who?** *person*   **How?** *method/manner/way*

13 Underline or highlight the *Wh-* question words and the other key words in these questions and say what kind of answer they require.

	Type of information
Which street is the bookshop situated in?	*name of street*
When is Sarah going to the restaurant?	**a** ....
Where can you see paintings by Van Gogh?	**b** ....
How many people were at the concert?	**c** ....
Why did Rudi telephone his mother?	**d** ....
What did the Customs Officer find in the man's bag?	**e** ....
Who came to the party?	**f** ....
What happened to the old lady?	**g** ....
How did the student hurt his foot?	**h** ....

How are Type 2 questions marked?
In this type of short answer question, you will have to make a list of up to three things. Note the question numbers as this will tell you how many marks they are worth.

Look at these example questions to see how many marks each one is worth.

> *Question 17*
> *Name **TWO** places where you can see paintings by Van Gogh.*

There is only one question, so you need both answers for one mark.

> *Questions 18–20*
> *Name **THREE** things that the Customs Officer found in the man's bag.*

There are three questions, so you get one mark for each answer.

How should I write my answers?
Write the correct words and/or numbers on the answer sheet. Use no more words than you are told to use and make sure you spell them correctly. You can write numbers in words or figures.

ACTION PLAN

▶ Check the instructions to see how many words you can write in your answer.

▶ Check to see if all the questions follow the same format.

▶ Underline or highlight the key words in each question and decide what kind of information you need to listen out for.

▶ As you listen, write your answers.

NOW TRY THE TASK

((◀ *Listen to Extract 3. (CD Track 5)*

Answer the questions below.

Write **NO MORE THAN THREE WORDS** *for each answer.*

Questions 14 and 15

14 On which level is the new section located?

....

15 What does the Gallery exhibit besides paintings?

....

Question 16

16 Name **TWO** things which accompany
the special exhibitions.

....

....

17 How does question 16 differ from questions 14 and 15?

RECORDING SCRIPT PAGE 117
ANSWERS PAGE 108
PRACTICE TEST PAGE 93

Listening Section 3

These are the Question Types you will practise here

MULTIPLE CHOICE

MATCHING

LABELLING A DIAGRAM

Section 1	Conversation (two speakers)	Social/survival	e.g. booking a hotel
Section 2	Talk by one speaker	General	e.g. radio talk
Section 3	**Discussion (two to four speakers)**	**Educational**	**e.g. tutorial discussion**
Section 4	Talk or lecture by one speaker	Course-related	e.g. university lecture

What is Section 3 like?

You will hear a discussion with up to four speakers on an educational topic. Section 3 is more difficult than Sections 1 and 2. You will have to follow the discussion and listen for important facts, reasons or ideas. You may also have to identify views or opinions.

How can I follow the discussion?

1 Look at part of a discussion with three speakers. What is the logical order for them to speak in?

A *Is it that old? I hadn't realised that.*

C *No. A lot of people don't realise that, but I still think ancient Egyptian art is more interesting than rock art.*

B *Much Australian Aboriginal rock art is more than 40,000 years old; that's five times older than the Egyptian pyramids.*

2 Now look at this discussion with three speakers, one of whom speaks twice. What order should they speak in?

A *Aren't there two main types of tea: green and black?*

B *I believe it comes from the dried leaves of a small tree called a camellia bush. It's mostly grown in sub-tropical areas like Sri Lanka, Japan and China.*

C *Where do we get tea from?*

D *Yes. You're right. Green tea is picked and dried quickly, which is what gives it a mild flavour. That's why it's very popular in China and Japan.*

3 Do any of the speakers in either discussion give a personal opinion?

4 Which of the speakers in either discussion state a fact or give a reason?

How can I pick out important facts, ideas or reasons?

You need to listen to what the speakers ask or tell each other, and then decide what their main point is. Sometimes you have to understand how the idea has been re-worded in the questions.

5 Read the following exchanges A and B, and choose the correct sentence endings from the boxes.

A **Student**
Are there any areas of my work that you think I could improve?

Tutor *Well, your work's been pretty good this term. I like the way you set out your data. You could perhaps learn a bit more about the topic, that's the only thing. But you obviously pay attention in lectures.*

The student needs to work on his
i concentration.
ii presentation skills.
iii subject knowledge.

B **Student**
Oh hi, I can't find Mr Peterson. Is he on holiday?

Administrator *Actually he's just back from two weeks' study leave but he's not here today. He seems to have developed a nasty cold. Try joining his four o'clock class tomorrow. He should be back by then.*

Mr Peterson is unavailable because he is
i off sick.
ii on study leave.
iii teaching another class.

6 Read the following exchanges A, B and C, and decide whether the speakers agree with each other or not.

A *A camel's hump contains water so that it can go without drinking for many days, doesn't it?*

I'm not so sure. I think it's made of fat, which can be converted to energy and water. But I don't think it actually contains water.

B *It's awful when people throw rubbish and cigarette butts in the street and just expect someone else to clean it up. It's really so lazy!*

You have a point. It is lazy of them. But if we had more public rubbish bins, that might help too.

C *If you want to lose weight, you should cut out fats and carbohydrates; things like potatoes, rice, pasta... and just eat meat and vegetables.*

That's all very well but it's not very healthy. You need carbohydrates to give you energy. Personally, I think it's better to try to have a balanced diet.

Question Types and Practice Tasks

MULTIPLE CHOICE

You choose the correct answer to a question from three options (A, B or C).

What is multiple choice?

There are two types of multiple choice questions, and you can get both types together in the same set of questions.

A question followed by three possible options.

How was the project funded?	The project was funded by
A by the government	**A** the government.
B by the university	**B** the university.
C by raising money	**C** raising money.

An unfinished statement followed by three possible endings.

How should I write my answers?

You only need to write the correct letter A, B or C on the answer sheet.

ACTION PLAN

▶ Read what is given carefully and note whether it is a question or a statement.
▶ Underline or highlight the key words.
▶ Re-phrase the question or statement in your own words.
▶ Read the three possible answers and underline or highlight the key words.
▶ Try to re-phrase the possible answers in your own words.
▶ As you listen, choose the correct answer.

NOW TRY THE TASK

((▶ *Listen to Extract 1. (CD Track 6)*

Question 7

Choose the correct letter A, B or C.

7 Why do flamingos in captivity need to eat algae?
   A to ensure they remain healthy
   B to supplement their diet
   C to keep their bodies pink

8 How did you re-phrase the three options?

9 Can you explain why two of the options are not correct?

RECORDING SCRIPT PAGE 118

MATCHING

You answer the questions by matching the words in the list (1, 2, 3, etc.) to the correct word or phrase in the box (A, B, C, etc.). There may not be a match for every item in the box, and you may need to use some items in the box more than once.

What is matching?

You will see a list of numbered questions and a list of options labelled with a letter. You match the correct option to each question based on what you hear.

A requires stamina	*takes a lot of energy*
B played worldwide	....
C potentially dangerous	....
D extremely popular	....
E expensive equipment	....
F easy to learn	....
G exciting to watch	....

10 Look at the list of options A–G and re-write the phrases in your own words. Describe each sport (1–5) using some of your alternative expressions.

1 table tennis
2 cycling
3 snowboarding
4 basketball
5 football

How should I write my answers?

You only need to write the correct letters A, B, C, etc. on the answer sheet.

ACTION PLAN

▶ Look at the list of numbered questions and decide what they have in common.
▶ Say them quietly to yourself to help you recognise them on the recording.
▶ Read the list of options, noting any heading in the box.
▶ Re-phrase each of the options in your own words.
▶ As you listen, match the options to the questions.

NOW TRY THE TASK

Questions 11–14

What does the lecturer say about each student?
*Choose FOUR answers from the box and write the correct letters **A–G** next to questions 11–14.*

> *David's work was good but lacked content. The paper would be better if it included some more examples but there's no need for him to re-submit.*

> *Lee's research is groundbreaking and of a very high standard. I don't have any concerns about him.*

> *Kim's work hasn't been assessed yet, so I'm not in a position to comment.*

> *Rosa's work is usually pretty good, though certainly not brilliant. She deserves a solid pass.*

Comments on students' work

A needs to re-submit
B reasonable level throughout
C still to be marked
D shows potential
E needs more data
F excellent original work
G below average

11 David .... 13 Lee ....

12 Rosa .... 14 Kim ....

15 Underline or highlight the words in the speech bubbles that match the answers for this task.

LABELLING A DIAGRAM

You label the parts on a diagram using up to three words and/or a number. The parts to be labelled will have an arrow and the question number beside them. You may have a box of possible answers to choose from.

What sort of diagram will I have to label?

You may have a diagram illustrating a process or you may have to label parts of an object. The parts to be labelled will be clearly indicated.

How should I write my answers?

If you have a box of options, you only need to write the correct answer A, B, C, etc. Otherwise you write the words you hear on the recording. Only use the number of words you are told to use and remember to spell them correctly.

ACTION PLAN

▶ Read the instructions to see how many words you can write in your answer.
▶ Look carefully at the diagram and decide what it is about.
▶ Note any title or labels already included.
▶ If you have a box of possible answers, read the words in the box and think about how they relate to the diagram.
▶ Think about where the labels might go or what the unlabelled parts might be.
▶ As you listen, choose an answer from the box or the recording.

NOW TRY THE TASK

((◀ *Listen to Extract 2. (CD Track 7)*

Questions 16–18

Label the diagram below.
*Choose three answers from the box and write the correct letters **A–G** next to questions 16–18.*

A metal frame

B wing

C plastic cells

D door

E computer

F road map

G camera

16 ....

17 ....

18 ....

Prototype for a plastic car

multi-directional wheels

RECORDING SCRIPT PAGE 118
ANSWERS PAGE 108
PRACTICE TEST PAGE 94

Listening Section 4

Section 1	Conversation (two speakers)	Social/survival	e.g. booking a hotel
Section 2	Talk by one speaker	General	e.g. radio talk
Section 3	Discussion (two to four speakers)	Educational	e.g. tutorial discussion
Section 4	**Talk or lecture by one speaker**	**Course-related**	**e.g. university lecture**

What is Section 4 like?

You will hear a lecture or talk based on a course-related topic. Section 4 is the hardest section of the test. The question types are similar to those in Sections 1–3, but you will have to follow the development of the lecture and identify the main ideas or key points.

How is a lecture usually structured?

The language is quite formal. The speaker usually begins by telling the listeners what he or she is going to say and then the main points are clearly identified, often illustrated with examples.

Today, I'm going to talk about the role of computers in early education. Firstly we'll look at keyboard skills and young children.

How can I follow the lecture and predict what I might hear?

Look carefully at the vocabulary in the questions and listen out for 'signpost' words used during the talk, e.g. *firstly, on the other hand, one way is*, as these will help you predict what the speaker is going to say. The words given will help you predict what is coming.

1 Look at the signpost words 1–10, which signal different kinds of information. Match the words in the box with the meanings a–j.

1 One way...
2 In fact...
3 And... in addition
4 Surprisingly enough...
5 By contrast...
6 Lastly...
7 Let's move on to...
8 Generally speaking,...
9 In other words,...
10 On the other hand,...

a another example
b something that is unexpected
c making the point clearer by giving supporting information
d something quite different / the opposite
e a closing statement or final point in a list
f a possible action that can produce the result you want
g a change of subject
h most of the time, usually
i providing an opposing point of view
j re-stating something in a different way

A Not many people actually voted at the last election. ...., the figures indicated that less than half of the eligible voters turned out on the day.

B Some people argue that exercise is the key to good health. ...., if you don't take exercise, you don't run the risk of injuring yourself!

C Basically there are two approaches to writing. .... is to make some notes before you begin, and the other is to dive in without a plan. But for academic writing, we definitely recommend the first.

D We've been through all the main points, so ...., I'd like to wish you all good luck with the exam.

E There are various views on the causes of pollution, but ...., it is felt that burning fossil fuels is mostly to blame.

F You'd think that learning a foreign alphabet would be difficult but ...., it's not so hard once you get started.

2 Complete the speech bubbles A–F with the most appropriate signpost words from the box on page 25. There may be more than one possibility.

Question Types and Practice Tasks

NOTE COMPLETION

You complete the notes by writing no more than three words and/or a number in the gap. Some of the information may already be completed to help you.

What does note completion involve?

You complete the notes with the words you hear on the recording. Notes may not follow standard grammatical rules or layout, e.g. there may be articles or auxiliary verbs missing, or the notes may be lists with bullet points.

How can I tell where the answers are in the recording?

The words included in the task can guide you through the recording, so it is important to read all the notes in the task carefully during your reading time.

3 Read through the set of notes below and decide what the topic is. Use your own words to form a question for each gap.

4 Work out what type of information is needed to complete the notes below, e.g. *an object, a number*, etc.

((◆ *Listen to Extract 1 (CD Track 8) and check your predictions with the recording script on page 118.*

String of human DNA
- approximately three feet long
- looks like a (5) ....
- includes between 50,000 and 100,000 genes

Complete set known as the human genome
Is very similar to many (6) .... and ....

How should I write my answers?
Write the correct words and/or numbers on the answer sheet. Use no more words than you are told to use and make sure you spell them correctly. You can write numbers in words or figures.

ACTION PLAN

▶ Read the instructions carefully to see how many words you can write.
▶ Look at the layout of the task, e.g. bullet points or continuous notes.
▶ Read the notes and decide what the topic is.
▶ Try to re-phrase the notes to form a question in your own words for each gap.
▶ Underline or highlight the key words around each gap and use these to help you listen for the answer.
▶ Note whether there is more than one gap for any of the questions.
▶ As you listen, complete the notes.

NOW TRY THE TASK

((◗ *Listen to Extract 2. (CD Track 9)*

Questions 7–9
Complete the notes below.
*Write **NO MORE THAN THREE WORDS** for each answer.*

Lonely Planet

– head office located in **(7)** .... but branches worldwide

– uses a variety of **(8)** .... to be competitive
    e.g. – tracking customers
            – allowing name to be used by a **(9)** ....

RECORDING SCRIPT PAGE 118

FLOW CHART COMPLETION

A flow chart always represents a sequence of events or a process. You complete the flow chart by writing up to three words and/or a number in the gaps. You may have a box of possible answers to choose from.

What is flow chart completion?
Flow chart completion is like note completion. It may not follow standard grammatical rules or layout.

How should I write my answers?
Write the correct words and/or numbers on the answer sheet. Use no more words than you are told to use and make sure you spell them correctly. You can write numbers in words or figures.

ACTION PLAN

▶ Look carefully at the questions and decide what the overall topic is.
▶ Note how the sequence works.
▶ Decide what type of word is needed to fill the gaps, e.g. a noun or a verb.
▶ As you listen, complete the flow chart.

NOW TRY THE TASK

(((▶ *Listen to Extract 3. (CD Track 10)*

Questions 10–13
Complete the flow chart below.
Write **NO MORE THAN THREE WORDS** *for each answer.*

Olive oil production

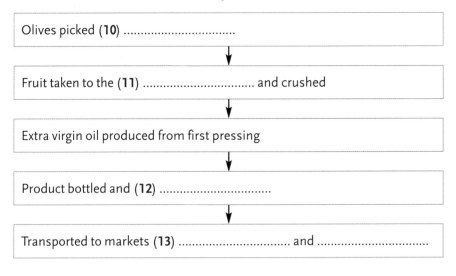

> Olives picked (**10**) ....

> Fruit taken to the (**11**) .... and crushed

> Extra virgin oil produced from first pressing

> Product bottled and (**12**) ....

> Transported to markets (**13**) .... and ....

Signpost words
- after this initial process
- then
- finally
- the first step is to
- incidentally

14 Look at the box of signpost words and put them in the order that best fits the information in the flow chart above, then listen to Extract 3 again.

RECORDING SCRIPT PAGE 118

CLASSIFICATION

You decide which category some words or statements belong to. The categories are usually A, B, C, etc. The words or statements are usually the questions.

What does classification involve?

A classification task has a list of options labelled A, B, C, etc. Based on what you hear, you match the words or ideas in the questions to one of the options.

15 Look at the example below and decide what the topic is. Read the question and note how it relates to the numbered items and options A–C.

Which method works best for the following materials?

A burying	1	aluminium	....
B burning	2	glass	....
C recycling	3	plastics	....
	4	paper	....
	5	green waste	....

16 What do the words A–C refer to?

How should I write my answers?

You only need to write the correct letter A, B, C, etc. on the answer sheet.

ACTION PLAN

▶ Look at the task and decide what the topic is.
▶ Look at the main question and the numbered items that follow it.
▶ Look at the numbered items and decide what they have in common.
▶ Look at the words A, B, C, etc. and decide how they relate to the question.
▶ As you listen, decide which letter best fits each numbered item.

NOW TRY THE TASK

((▶ *Listen to Extract 4. (CD Track 11)*

Questions 17–21

According to the speaker, which method works best for mastering these skills?

*Write the correct letters **A–C** next to questions 17–21.*

A language laboratory	17	speaking	....
B self-study	18	listening	....
C small group work	19	pronunciation	....
	20	grammar	....
	21	reading	....

RECORDING SCRIPT PAGE 118
ANSWERS PAGE 109
PRACTICE TEST PAGE 95

The Academic Reading Test

A 60-minute test of your reading skills

How many sections does the reading test have?
There are three sections in the reading test. Each section consists of a reading passage and 13 or 14 questions. There are 40 questions in total. The whole test lasts an hour and you are advised to spend 20 minutes on each section. Altogether you have to read a maximum of 2750 words.

Is there any difference between the sections?
The only difference is that Section 1 may be a little easier than the other sections. There is no other difference.

What is the reading test like?
You will receive an answer sheet, and a reading test booklet with the passages and questions in it. Each passage will be on a different topic.

Where do I write my answers?

IELTS reading passages are long – each one is about 900 words.

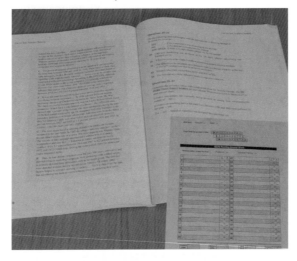

You can write on the question booklet but you must write all your final answers on the reading answer sheet.

📄 ON THE DAY

- The reading test is the second part of the IELTS test, held after the listening test on the same day.

- The supervisor will write the start and finish times on the board, and give you a ten-minute warning before the end.

- You must write your answers in pencil on the answer sheet.

- Unlike the listening test, there is no transfer time. After one hour, the test is over and you must hand in the answer sheet.

What topics will I find in the reading passages?
The topics are of general interest but related to an academic subject. They often deal with global issues, such as the environment, language, conservation, tourism, etc.

Will I be able to understand the passages?
Although the topics may seem unfamiliar to you, none of the passages will contain technical information or specialist vocabulary that is not explained or cannot be understood by an educated reader. Sometimes, however, you will need to ignore unknown words or guess their meaning.

What sort of questions will I get?
There are many different question types in the reading test (see pages 32–3). Often you have to choose the correct letter or write some words. If you have to write an answer, you will never have to use more than three words and/or a number.

Will I get every question type in the test?
No. Each section of the test usually contains two to four question types, so in one complete reading test you could get a maximum of 12 different question types. (Usually you will get about eight or nine.) Sometimes the same question type occurs in more than one section of the test. Remember, you may get a mix of the reading question types in any section of the test.

Why are there different reading question types?
IELTS tests a range of reading skills that you need for study purposes. For example, if a passage has eight paragraphs, each with a clear theme, then you may get paragraph heading questions that test whether or not you can identify the main theme of each paragraph. If a passage contains a lot of detailed information, you may get sentence completion questions that ask you to find specific information.

These are the main skills that IELTS tests:
• reading quickly to get a general idea or find a particular word
• finding detailed or factual information
• understanding themes and main ideas
• identifying views, arguments and claims
• identifying the overall theme of the passage.

What general approach should I take to the reading test?
Do the sections in the order they come. Read the title and sub-heading (if there is one) of each passage and use these to form an idea of what the passage is about. Then read quickly through the questions and note what type they are. Read the passage quickly before you start doing the questions to see how the topic is developed and note the main ideas. Start with the first set of questions. When you go on to the second set of questions, you may have to go back to the start of the passage to find the answers.

How can I improve my score in the reading test?
You can help improve your score by making sure that you know what each question type tests and by having a general approach for each set of questions. The following pages, divided into three sections, provide you with an **Action Plan** for each set of questions.

What else can I do to prepare for the reading test?
You should read as widely as you can and practise reading quickly to get the main ideas. You should also familiarise yourself with ideas and vocabulary related to topics of global interest or concern.

How is the reading test marked?
There is one mark per question and this makes a total of 40 marks. Your mark is converted into a Band Score of between 1 and 9. You can get half bands in the reading test, e.g. 6.5.

Is correct spelling important?
Your spelling must be correct and your handwriting must be clear. The answers must come from the reading passages, and you will lose marks if you copy words incorrectly. You should not use abbreviations unless they are in the passage, and you should check plurals.

Overview of the Academic Reading Question Types

Question type	Action	Key points	Page
Sentence completion	You complete the gaps in the sentences using words from the passage.	• Answers are in passage order. • Write up to three words and/or a number. • Check spelling with passage. • Check grammar of completed sentence. • Don't include any unnecessary words.	34
Notes / table / flow chart completion	You complete the gaps in the notes, table or flow chart using words from the passage.	• Answers may not be in passage order. • Write up to three words and/or a number. • Check spelling with passage. • Don't include any unnecessary words.	36
Short answer questions	You answer the questions using words from the passage.	• Answers are in passage order. • Write up to three words and/or a number. • Check spelling with passage. • Don't include any unnecessary words.	37
Labelling a diagram	You name parts of a diagram using words from the passage.	• Answers may not be in passage order. • Write up to three words and/or a number. • Check spelling with passage. • Don't include any unnecessary words. • Mark relevant parts of passage while reading.	38
True / False / Not Given	You decide whether the statement agrees with or contradicts the passage, or whether there is no information.	• Answers are in passage order. • Write True, False or Not Given.	39
Global multiple choice	You decide what the main theme of the passage is.	• Question covers whole passage. • Write A, B, C or D. • Check other options are wrong.	41
Matching	You match statements to items in a box.	• Statements are not in passage order. • Boxed items are usually in passage order. • Write A, B, C, etc. • Some letters may be used more than once. • Some letters may not be used.	42
Finding information in paragraphs	You find the paragraph that contains the information in the question.	• Write A, B, C, etc. • Some letters may be used more than once. • Some paragraphs may not be tested.	44

Overview of the Academic Reading Question Types

Question type	Action	Key points	Page
Sentence completion with a box	You complete the sentences by selecting the correct ending from a box of options.	• Answers are in passage order. • Write A, B, C, etc. • Some letters may not be used. • Check grammar and meaning of sentence.	45
Yes / No / Not Given	You decide whether the statement agrees with or contradicts the writer's views or claims, or whether there is no information.	• Answers are in passage order. • Write Yes, No or Not Given.	47
Multiple choice	You choose the correct letter A, B, C or D.	• Answers are in passage order. • Write A, B, C or D. • Check other options are wrong.	49
Paragraph headings	You choose the correct heading for each paragraph from a list of headings.	• Underline or highlight main ideas in paragraphs. • Write the correct number i, ii, iii, etc. • Some headings will not be used.	50
Summary completion	You complete the gaps in the summary using words from the passage.	• Answers may not be in passage order. • Write up to three words and/or a number. • Check spelling with passage. • Check grammar of completed summary. • Don't include any unnecessary words.	52
Summary completion with a box	You complete the gaps in the summary using words or phrases from a box.	• Answers may not be in passage order. • Write A, B, C, etc. • Some letters will not be used. • Check spelling with passage. • Check grammar of completed summary.	54
Classification	You decide which category some statements or features belong to.	• Answers are not in passage order. • Write A, B, C, etc. • Some letters may be used more than once. • Some letters may not be used.	55
Pick from a list	You pick the correct answers from a list of options.	• Answers may not be in passage order. • Write A, B, C, etc. • Each answer may score one mark or the whole question may score one mark.	57

These are the Question
Types you will practise here

SENTENCE COMPLETION
NOTES / TABLE / FLOW
   CHART COMPLETION
SHORT ANSWER QUESTIONS
LABELLING A DIAGRAM
TRUE / FALSE / NOT GIVEN
GLOBAL MULTIPLE CHOICE

▶▶▶▶▶▶▶▶▶▶▶▶▶▶▶▶▶▶

Academic Reading Section 1

Section 1	13 questions	One passage	Approx 900 words
Section 2	13 questions	One passage	Approx 900 words
Section 3	14 questions	One passage	Approx 900 words

Question Types and Practice Tasks

SENTENCE COMPLETION
You complete the sentences by writing up to three words and/or a number from the passage in the gaps. The gaps can come at the beginning, in the middle or at the end of the sentence. The answers are in passage order.

What is involved in sentence completion questions?
You need to try to predict the kind of words that are missing before you look for the answers.

Read the sentences below and decide what type of information is missing, e.g. place name, date, noun, adjective, etc. Make a note in the box.
1 .... is the date of the next proposed mission to Mars.
2 The astronauts that walk on the moon are going to need specially designed .... for their mission.
3 Compared to the moon, Mars is considered to be ....

1 ....

2 ....

3 ....

How should I write my answers?
You should only use words from the passage, and you must use no more words than you are told to use. They should be written exactly as they are in the reading passage (numbers too) and they have to be spelt correctly. Do not include unnecessary words, or repeat words that are already provided in the sentence.

ACTION PLAN

▶ Read the instructions carefully to see how many words you can write.
▶ Note the position of the gaps in the sentences.
▶ Start with the first question and decide what kind of word(s) is/are needed to complete the sentence.
▶ Note any grammatical clues, e.g. articles or prepositions, which may help you find the answer.
▶ Underline or highlight the key words around each gap and use these to find the right part of the passage.
▶ Decide exactly which words or numbers you should write as the answer.
▶ Read the completed sentence to make sure that it is grammatically correct and makes sense.

NOW TRY THE TASK

Complete the sentences below.
*Choose **NO MORE THAN THREE WORDS** from the passage for each answer.*

Power-packed fliers

For their size, birds are tremendously powerful creatures. We know this thanks to an ingenious series of tests performed by researchers at Duke University in North Carolina. The researchers placed a specially trained budgerigar in a wind tunnel and measured how much muscle power it needed to maintain flight at various airspeeds up to 50 kilometres per hour. The small bird had to be trained, not only because it had to fly in the artificial environment of the wind tunnel, but also because it had to do so while wearing a tiny oxygen mask.

The mask allowed zoologist Vance Tucker and his colleagues to monitor the budgerigar's oxygen demand, and thus the amount of mechanical energy it was producing. What they discovered was experimental proof of the incredible power-to-weight ratio of birds. Tucker's team found that the 35-gram budgerigar's flight muscles were delivering a peak power of one to four watts to maintain continuous flight. That might not sound very much on its own, but it's pretty impressive when the bird's size is taken into account: it works out as 200 watts of continuous mechanical power for every kilogram of the bird's muscle mass.

And that's the reason that people have always failed when they tried to fly by flapping wings attached to their arms: the average human can only produce around ten watts per kilogram of their muscle mass. It's not that we never had the time to fly – we have simply never had the energy. To fly, people need machines and to make a flying machine, we need to understand how birds control their flight.

Type of word
4 *singular noun*
5 ....
6 ....
7 ....

Complete the table on the left first to help you predict the answers.

4 Scientists have done experiments on birds in a ....

5 The birds reached a maximum hourly flight distance of ....

6 The aim of scientists was to calculate the amount of .... they needed to fly.

7 .... are the only solution to human flight.

8 Why would these answers be marked wrong?
   a tunnel / a wind tunnel (Q4)
   b 50 kilomitres / 50 kilometres per hour (Q5)
   c oxygen demand / watts (Q6)
   d flying machine / flapping wings (Q7)

▶▶▶▶▶▶▶▶▶▶▶▶▶▶▶▶▶▶▶

NOTES / TABLE / FLOW CHART COMPLETION

You complete the gaps in the notes, table or flow chart using up to three words and/or a number from the passage. Some of the information may already be completed to help you. The answers may not be in passage order.

Press a switch and immediately a light comes on or an electrical machine springs into action. This is because your home is automatically supplied with electricity that runs from a power station, where it is produced, through power lines to the wires and electrical circuits in the floors, ceilings and walls of your home.

How are these question types different from sentence completion?
The questions are not full sentences, so you need not worry about the grammatical correctness of a sentence.

Read this paragraph and look at question 9.

9 A and B below test your understanding of the same piece of information. What is the difference between the two types of question and what is the correct answer for each?

A Electricity is generated in .... and is transported by power lines to homes.

B Electricity: generated in ....
transported by power lines

ACTION PLAN

▶ Follow the Action Plan for sentence completion on page 34 and write your answers in the same way. If you are completing a table, look at the table headings to help you decide what sort of words to look for.

NOW TRY THE TASK

Complete the notes.
*Choose **NO MORE THAN TWO WORDS** from the passage for each answer.*

Notes

Research shows:
Need to train the ear to make it work well

Geographical research area:

10 ....

Examples of people with poor hearing:

11 ....

12 ....

and good hearing:

13 ....

14 ....

Most dangerous type of noise:

15 ....

❖◆ SILENCE IS NOT ALWAYS GOLDEN ◆❖

A global survey has found that city dwellers have better hearing than people who live in quiet villages, and scientists now believe that the ear needs exercise to keep in shape.

A team of scientists at the University of Giessen, Germany, has spent over a decade testing the hearing of more than 10,000 people around the world. As expected, people exposed to extremely loud noises at work, such as construction workers, had poor hearing. But the hearing of those living in quiet, rural areas, such as farmers, was just as bad. Orchestral musicians and airline pilots, by contrast, can usually hear well despite exposure to noise at work. And there is little difference between people who go to noisy concerts and those who do not.

Hearing specialists have long believed that prolonged exposure to excessively loud noise degrades hearing and so industrial standards are based on people's average exposure to sound energy. However, it is the very strong impulses, such as loud bangs, that do the most damage, whereas exposure to continual noise 'trains' the ear to tolerate it.

16 Find words in the passage that have a similar meaning to the highlighted words in the notes.

SHORT ANSWER QUESTIONS

You answer the questions using up to three words and/or a number from the passage. The answers are in passage order.

What is involved in short answer questions?

You need to underline or highlight the key words in the questions that tell you what kind of information to find and how much to write in your answer. These are often words like *when, who, how many, which,* etc.

Here is an example of key words in a question:
Which group of scientists does the writer criticize?

How should I write my answers?

You should only use words from the passage, and you must use no more words than you are told to use. They should be written exactly as they are in the reading passage (numbers too) and they have to be spelt correctly. Do not include unnecessary words.

ACTION PLAN

▶ Read the instructions carefully to see how many words you can write.
▶ Underline or highlight the key words in each question and decide what kind of information you need to look for.
▶ Start with the first question and read the passage quickly to see if you can find words that are the same as the key words or have a similar meaning.
▶ Read around these words to find the answer.
▶ Decide exactly which words and/or numbers you should write as the answer.

NOW TRY THE TASK

Answer the questions below.
*Choose **NO MORE THAN THREE WORDS** from the passage for each answer.*

> From the earliest times, people have devised highly ingenious methods for conserving water where it is scarce. In the Sahara in Africa, where two-thirds of the sparse population live in permanent settlements, many of the oases that provide natural supplies of water have been enlarged by human industry. In some places, gently sloping channels called foggaras run below the surface, collecting ground water that flows to a central oasis. In other places, artesian wells are used to irrigate date palms and other crops that grow in the shade they provide. In Egypt, only one per cent of all water enters the domestic supply. The remainder is used to irrigate farm crops.

Answer must be a place – perhaps geographical, perhaps a building, perhaps an area.

17 Where do many people in the Sahara have their homes? *Permanent*

18 What water sources in the Sahara have people developed? *OASIS*

19 What land constructions are used for irrigation purposes in the Sahara? *Wells*

20 Which African crop is mentioned? *Palms*

21 How much of the water in Egypt is used by people in their homes? *One Percent*

22 Which words did you highlight in the questions?

LABELLING A DIAGRAM

You name parts of a diagram using up to three words and/or a number from the passage. The parts to be labelled will have an arrow and the question number beside them. The answers may not be in passage order. However, the answers are usually grouped together in one part of the passage, where the diagram is described.

How should I write my answers?

You should only use words from the passage, and you must use no more words than you are told to use. They should be written exactly as they are in the reading passage (numbers too) and they have to be spelt correctly.

ACTION PLAN

▶ Read the instructions carefully to see how many words you can write.
▶ Look at the diagram to form a general idea of the content.
▶ Note any labels provided already, as these can help you find the answer.
▶ Look at the parts of the diagram to be labelled and decide what kind of information is needed to fill the gap, e.g. a place, a process, etc.
▶ Pay particular attention to expressions of place such as *in the middle*, *in the corner*, *beyond this*, *next to*, *above/below*, *leads to*, etc., as the answer to the questions may depend on your understanding these concepts.

NOW TRY THE TASK

Label the diagram below.
*Choose **NO MORE THAN THREE WORDS** from the passage for each answer.*

Zinacantan

The rural village of Zinacantan, situated high in the hills of southern Mexico, is inhabited by people descended from the ancient Mayans. The villages of this area are unique and interesting in terms of their traditions and lifestyle. A typical house has only two rooms: one large room, which serves as both a living room and a bedroom, and a small kitchen leading off this room. A typical home would have a row of beds along one wall, and three or four chairs in the middle of the room from which the family can watch the television. In the kitchen there is an open fire in the centre of the room, a bench for grinding corn and two large storage bins in the corner. A wide variety of crops are cultivated on the surrounding land, including herbs near the kitchen, and fruit trees beyond this. On the outer edge of the property the family would grow sugar cane.

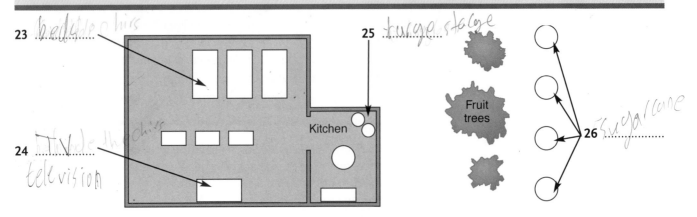

27 How many expressions of place can you find in the passage?

How do I know if the statement is true, false or not given?

True: The statement agrees with what is in the passage, i.e. says the same thing using different words.

False: The statement contradicts what is in the passage, i.e. says the opposite.

Not Given: There is no mention of this piece of information in the passage.

Read the article below and the three statements.
Look at the explanations and answers given in the boxes.

It was not John Landy who was the first to break this record (i.e. run a mile in under four minutes) but Roger Bannister. Statement A is therefore not True but False as it contradicts the passage.

The passage refers to the 50th anniversary of the event so the answer to statement B is True.

Although you may know this to be a fact, the passage does not say that Bannister was English, so the answer to statement C is Not Given.

The four-minute mile

One of the great sporting achievements of the 20th century was when the runner Roger Bannister broke the four-minute mile record. In being the first to do so, he denied his Australian rival, John Landy, the chance of achieving immortality in the field of athletics. Media interest in the 50th anniversary of the event, including the publication of two books on the subject, highlights the significance of the achievement.

A John Landy ran a mile in under four minutes before Roger Bannister.
B Fifty years have passed since the four-minute mile was broken.
C Roger Bannister was English.

How should I write my answers?
You only need to write T, F or NG. However, it is best to write the words in full so that your answer is clear.

ACTION PLAN

▶ Read the statements very carefully.
▶ Underline or highlight the key words or phrases in the first statement and quickly read the passage for these. Often you will find the same words, names or numbers in the passage. This is done to help you find the idea or information and get started in the right part of the passage.
▶ Read around the words in the passage and see whether the information agrees with the statement, contradicts it or whether nothing is said about it.
▶ Decide whether the answer is True, False or Not Given.

NOW TRY THE TASK

Do the following statements agree with the information given in the reading passage?
Write

TRUE　　　　*if the statement agrees with the information*
FALSE　　　　*if the statement contradicts the information*
NOT GIVEN　　*if there is no information on this*

> That is, there was a lot of interest in breaking the record.

● The race to break the four-minute mile reached a crescendo in the 1950s and became a major sporting challenge of the day. At the turn of the twentieth century, the world record had stood at about four minutes ten seconds. But despite efforts around the globe, by 1952 the record remained intact. The press regularly stated at that time that man had reached his athletic limits; that room for improvement was minimal. Then in May 1954, in a run that was to go down in history, Roger Bannister stopped the clock at 3 minutes 59.4 seconds.

Few records have so captured the public's attention and provided such an enduring benchmark. Public fascination partly reflected the seeming symmetry of the event – four laps in four minutes. A very similar achievement is that of the less well-known Russian swimmer Vladimir Salnikov, who in 1980 became the first man to break 15 minutes for 1500 metres. That was 30 consecutive laps in less than 30 seconds, which had once been regarded as impossible.

Part of the appeal of athletes such as Bannister and Landy is linked to the amateur environment in which they competed. For both men, running was an aside to the real matters of life and they received no monetary reward. And as evidence of the temporal nature of all records, Bannister's record has since been reduced by a further 17 seconds, but the four-minute mile remains a landmark in sporting history.

28 In the mid 20th century, there was little interest in breaking the four-minute mile.

29 In the early 1950s, the media promoted the idea that nobody could run a mile in under four minutes. *F*

30 In 1980, Vladimir Salnikov swam 1500 metres in less than 15 minutes. *T*

31 John Landy and Roger Bannister were professional sportsmen. *F*

32 Bannister's record was broken within three years. *F*

33 Complete the table below to show how you found your answers. *NG*

	Phrases in the question that **help you find the part of the passage** where the answer is	Phrases in the passage that **match** these	Phrases in the passage that **tell you the answer**	KEY
28	in the mid 20th century	in the 1950s	became a major sporting challenge	False
29				
30				
31				
32				

GLOBAL MULTIPLE CHOICE
You decide what the main idea/theme/topic of the passage is, or why the passage was written, or choose a suitable title for the passage. These questions usually come at the end. Often the passage will not have a title if it has a global multiple choice question.

How should I write my answers?
Write A, B, C or D.

ACTION PLAN

▶ Underline or highlight the key words in the question and the four options.
▶ Quickly read the sentences that contain the main ideas in each paragraph of the passage.
▶ Rule out any options in the questions that you think are definitely wrong.
▶ Decide which option is correct.

NOW TRY THE TASK

*Choose the correct letter **A**, **B**, **C** or **D**.*

34 Why was the article on page 40 written?
    A to show the overall improvement in sporting achievements
    B to illustrate an important event in the world of sport
    C to encourage young people to participate in sport
    D to compare running and swimming world records

35 Why are the other options attractive, but wrong?

ANSWERS PAGE 109
PRACTICE TEST PAGE 96

These are the Question
Types you will practise here

MATCHING

FINDING INFORMATION
   IN PARAGRAPHS

SENTENCE COMPLETION
   WITH A BOX

YES / NO / NOT GIVEN

MULTIPLE CHOICE

▶▶▶▶▶▶▶▶▶▶▶▶▶▶▶▶▶▶▶

Academic Reading Section 2

Section 1	13 questions	One passage	Approx 900 words
Section 2	**13 questions**	**One passage**	**Approx 900 words**
Section 3	14 questions	One passage	Approx 900 words

Question Types and Practice Tasks

MATCHING

You match statements to items in a box. The statements are usually
numbered 1, 2, 3, etc. and the items in the box are usually labelled A, B, C,
etc. There may not be a matching statement for every item in the box,
while you may need to use some items in the box more than once. The
items in the box are usually in passage order, but the statements are in
random order.

What sort of things can be matched?

There are many possibilities but matching people to statements is the most
common. You may also have to match things like features to languages,
historical events to dates, teaching methods to educational programmes, etc.

How should I write my answers?

You only need to write the correct letter A, B or C, etc. There is only ONE
answer for each question. You may use any letter more than once.

ACTION PLAN

▶ Start with the items in the box because these are usually in passage order.
   Underline or highlight these in the passage. Some of the items may appear
   more than once in the passage, so it is important to find them all.

▶ Carefully read the statements and mark the key words.

▶ Read around the first item (A) you have marked in the passage and read the
   list of statements quickly to see whether any of them matches. If A occurs in
   other parts of the passage, read around these parts too.

▶ Write the letter A next to the correct statement(s).

▶ Repeat this procedure with the next item in the boxed list.

▶ If you think two items fit any of the statements, you will need to come back
   to these, as there is only one answer for each statement.

NOW TRY THE TASK

Look at the following statements (Questions 1–5) and the list of people below.
*Match each statement with the correct person **A–D**.*

✶✶ Effective advertising ✶✶

In recent years, advertising has been more preoccupied with grabbing attention and sustaining interest than with transferring persuasive messages. According to Sean Brierley, this has largely been due to a perception that advertising needed to stand out and appeal through humorous, artistic or educational content in order to be well received by consumers. The agencies who produced these kinds of commercials argued that, because there was so little product difference, advertisers needed to provide difference through the advertising.

Others attacked this view: 'Advertising used to be about persuading people to want your product. Now the task seems to be to make people admire your advertising,' complained one industry commentator (Wilkins 1998).

This kind of debate is not new. Rosser Reeves called 'art' advertising on the TV in the 1950s 'vampire video', arguing that it distracts the viewer from the product and makes the commercial's selling message less effective.

Brierley notes that the debate around 'effective' advertising became much more intense in the 1990s with increases in media costs and declining sales. Other experts also pointed out that consumers were less naïve and more professional and cynical than they had been. Being more aware of the process of manufacturing, marketing and communication, it was felt that 'a conclusion which the viewer has reached himself will last longer and be better internalised' (Lannon 1993).

That is, it has to attract our attention and be amusing.

A Brierley
B Wilkins
C Reeves
D Lannon

1 It is unfortunate that the focus of advertising has changed.
2 Reduced profits was one reason why advertisements changed.
3 Consumers need to feel they have made their own decisions.
4 A heavy focus on the advertisement, rather than the product, is unsuccessful.
5 These days we expect advertisements to be attractive and entertain us.

6 The answer to question 1 is B. How are the key words in the statement expressed in the passage?

▶▶▶▶▶▶▶▶▶▶▶▶▶▶▶▶▶

FINDING INFORMATION IN PARAGRAPHS

You find the paragraph that contains the information in the question. You may have to find a detail, an idea, a comparison, an example, etc. Some paragraphs may contain the information required in more than one question, while other paragraphs may not be tested.

How is this question different from paragraph headings?

Paragraph headings test your understanding of the main idea in each paragraph, so the headings are the answers (see page 50). In this question type, you have to read the paragraphs to see whether they provide the information you need, so the paragraph letters are the answers. You need to use a different approach for this question type.

How should I write my answers?

You only need to write the correct paragraph letter A, B, C, etc. There is only ONE answer for each question.

ACTION PLAN

▶ Underline or highlight the key words in the questions.
▶ Think about the ideas and language that you need to look for.
▶ Read the first paragraph and then quickly read through the questions.
▶ Mark any parts of the paragraph that match the key words in the questions.
▶ Write the paragraph letter next to that question.
▶ Go on to the next paragraph and do the same.
▶ If you think a question can be matched to more than one paragraph, make a note of this and come back to the question later to make a decision.

NOW TRY THE TASK

*The reading passage has three paragraphs, **A–C**.*
Which paragraph contains the following information?

Dawn of modern man

A At first glance, the 41 perforated pea-sized shells found in a South African cave are merely ancient jewellery, albeit the oldest ever found. But to archaeologist Christopher Henshilwood, the 75,000-year-old beads represent symbolic thought. By wearing jewellery, the people living on the southern tip of Africa would have transmitted shared cultural values, much like we do today. 'The Blombos Cave beads present absolute evidence for perhaps the earliest storage of information outside the human brain,' he explains.

B They were originally located in layers of sand dating back to the Middle Stone Age, arranged in clusters of up to 17 beads of a similar size. Strong indications that they were used as jewellery come from wear-marks and the common position of holes. Traces of red ochre suggest that the beads, or the surfaces they had touched, were coated with pigment.

C The shells are those of a mollusc scavenger *Nassarius kraussianus*, which lives in estuaries. Since the nearest rivers to the cave are 20 km away, Stone Age humans must have transported them to the cave. The fact they were grouped into sizes and perforated suggests they were deliberately fashioned into beads, possibly before being taken there.

7 evidence that the shells had been worn
8 where in the cave the beads were first found
9 the type of creature that occupied the shells
10 a reference to the current function of jewellery
11 how it is thought the shells reached the cave

12 Which words in the passage match the key words in the statements?

SENTENCE COMPLETION WITH A BOX
You choose the correct ending from a box of options to make a complete sentence which contains an idea from the passage. There will be some extra endings that you do not need to use. You may be able to use some of the endings more than once. The answers are in passage order.

How is this different from sentence completion without a box?
In sentence completion without a box, you only have to find a detail in the passage and write the correct word or words to complete a sentence. Here, you have to join two parts of a sentence together to make one sentence that paraphrases an idea in the passage. You need to use a different approach for this question type so that the completed sentence makes logical sense and is grammatically correct.

13 Complete this sentence with the ending that is most likely to be correct.
Consumers are not inclined to cut back on waste because

> **A** they are hard to get rid of effectively.
> **B** there are no financial incentives to do this.
> **C** it is the only method available to them.

14 Explain why the other endings are wrong.

How should I write my answers?
You only need to write the correct letters A, B, C, etc. Usually the endings are only used once. If you need to use an ending more than once, the instructions will tell you.

ACTION PLAN

▶ Read the first unfinished statement carefully and underline or highlight the key words.
▶ Use the key words in the unfinished statement to find the idea in the passage.
▶ Read around the information in the passage to make sure you understand it.
▶ Quickly read the list of endings and underline or highlight the key words.
▶ Choose the ending which best fits the idea in the passage.
▶ Make sure the ending is logical and fits grammatically.

NOW TRY THE TASK

*Complete each sentence with the correct ending **A–G** below.*

Waste disposal

Until now, Britain has opted for burying most of its rubbish. Around four fifths of municipal waste is sent to landfill sites. This approach has made considerable sense in an island with sites to spare because of its particular geology and its history of quarrying.

But landfill sites are getting scarce, particularly in southern England, where most people live. And they are becoming expensive to run as the government insists on safeguards against environmental hazards like the leaching of toxic waste into underground aquefiers. But the biggest constraint on dumping stuff in landfill sites is Britain's commitment to meet European targets to slash the amount of biodegradable waste – about 60% of household rubbish – that is put into landfill sites. These targets are intended to cut emissions of methane (a greenhouse gas) and to reduce the risk of water contamination from landfill.

If you can't bury it, an alternative is to burn it. This certainly seemed to be the initial thrust of government thinking a few years ago. A programme to build as many as 130 new incinerators was envisaged. But burning also entails environmental risks. Although new incinerators are now much cleaner than earlier ones, people are scared of exposure to dangerous chemicals like cancer-producing dioxins. The political difficulties in selling an expansion of incineration are immense.

15 The presence of old mines in Britain has
16 To make landfill sites safer, the authorities have
17 In order to comply with European targets, Britain has
18 Burning rubbish is not popular because people have

A agreed to reduce waste levels.
B replaced old incinerators.
C destroyed most of the municipal waste.
D encouraged rubbish burial.
E released toxic waste.
F imposed safety laws.
G become anxious about the pollution levels.

YES / NO / NOT GIVEN

You decide whether the statement agrees with or contradicts the writer's views or claims, or whether there is no information relating to the statement in the passage. The answers are in passage order but they may be grouped together in one part of the passsage or spread across the passage.

How is this different from True / False / Not Given?

True / False / Not Given tests how well you understand factual information in the passage, whereas Yes / No / Not Given tests your understanding of the writer's views or claims. However, the approach to the two question types is the same.

What are the writer's views or claims?

Many passages include the writer's opinion (views or claims) on a topic as well as providing factual information.

19 Read this extract about security systems. Underline or highlight any views or claims made by the writer. Is the majority of the passage the writer's opinion or is it factual information?

The two sides to security · · · · · · · · · · · · · · · ·

In the security industry today, there are two clear divisions and one of these is decidedly more glamorous than the other. The glamorous part deals with digital security, which includes everything from fighting computer viruses and tackling malicious computer hackers to controlling which employees have access to which systems. All of this has overshadowed the less glamorous side of the industry, which deals with physical security – in essence, door locks, alarms and that sort of thing. The people involved in digital security come across as bright and interesting, whereas the door-lock people do not. This second group soon have to admit that there have been no real advances in locks since the invention of the pin-tumbler lock, which was actually devised in ancient Egypt but was then lost until Mr Linus Yale, an American inventor, rediscovered it. And even that was a century and a half ago.

How do I match the views to the statements?

The statements make one clear point. You decide whether they agree with or contradict the views expressed in the passage or whether the writer has given no information about that point.

Read the passage and the three statements below. Decide which one
  – agrees with the writer (Y)
  – contradicts the writer (N)
  – is based on information not found in the passage (NG).

20 Designing ways to protect computers from hackers represents the boring side of the security industry.

21 Conventional door-locking mechanisms have changed very little in the last century.

22 Linus Yale worked on the pin-tumbler lock alone.

What if I think I know the answer from my general knowledge?

You must only answer using the information you read in the passage. If you think you know the answer but it does not appear in the passage, the answer must be Not Given.

How should I write my answers?

You only need to write Y, N or NG. However, it is best to write the words in full so that your answer is clear.

ACTION PLAN

▶ Read the first statement carefully and re-phrase it in your own words.

▶ Underline or highlight the key words or phrases in the first statement and quickly read the passage for these. Often you will find the same words, names or numbers in the passage. This is done to help you find the idea or information and get started in the right part of the passage.

▶ Read around the words in the passage and see whether the view that is expressed agrees with the statement, contradicts it, or whether nothing is said about it.

NOW TRY THE TASK

Do the following statements agree with the claims of the writer in the passage below? Write

YES	*if the statement agrees with the information*
NO	*if the statement contradicts the information*
NOT GIVEN	*if there is no information on this*

23 It can be understood why people take their energy supplies for granted.
24 Some quite ordinary towns are developing green energy supplies.
25 Most people in need of electricity supplies live in poor countries.
26 The new high-tech industries will add to levels of unemployment.

๑ ๑ ๑ ๑ Blowing in the wind ๑ ๑ ๑ ๑

When all it takes is the flick of a switch to illuminate a house or to activate a television set, it is perhaps not surprising that most people pay little attention to where their energy comes from or what impact using it is having on the environment. But though the comfort and convenience of our modern energy supply is easy to accept, attitudes are beginning to change, partly because many people are starting to realise the scale of the impact we are having.

The potential for greener and cleaner energy sources is still greater than either demand or official backing, but momentum is gathering. Some two billion people are still without electricity, the majority of whom live in poor countries and in remote areas. In these conditions, local energy supplies based on renewable sources such as the wind or sun are the ideal solution. In richer countries, emerging energy sources could mean the foundation of new high-tech industries that employ hundreds of thousands of people.

27 Underline or highlight the words in the passage which gave you the answers.

MULTIPLE CHOICE

You choose the correct answer from four options (A,B,C or D). There are two types of multiple choice questions: Type 1 is a question followed by four possible options (which may or may not be full sentences) and Type 2 is an unfinished statement followed by four possible endings. You may get both types in the test. The answers are in passage order.

How should I write my answers?
You only need to write the correct letter (A, B, C or D).

ACTION PLAN

▶ Underline or highlight the key words in the question or unfinished statement.

▶ Match these key words to words in the passage so that you are looking in the right place for the answers.

▶ Underline or highlight the key words in the options and re-phrase the ideas in your mind.

▶ Read around the section of text you have marked and see if you can find words or expressions that match the options.

▶ Some word matches will occur, but check whether the passage is stating the same or something different from what is stated in the options.

NOW TRY THE TASK

*Choose the correct letter **A**, **B**, **C** or **D**.*

28 What does the writer say about the environmental impact of the work at Lake Magadi?

    A It has little effect on the area.
    B It has been going on too long.
    C It has been well planned.
    D It causes harm to the birds.

> Match key words in the question – especially names – to find the right part of the passage.

For more than 60 years, the Magadi Soda Company has been taking soda ash from Lake Magadi, south west of Nairobi, Kenya. The operation was set up without particular consideration for the natural environment but, over the years, it has proved harmless. The factory and town which might cause disturbance are located out of the way, about 15 kilometres from the area most densely populated by birds. The factory effluent consists only of returning lake water, and the gaseous emissions are only carbon dioxide and water.

29 Why are the other options attractive but wrong?

⚷ **ANSWERS PAGE 110**
    PRACTICE TEST PAGE 99

PARAGRAPH HEADINGS

SUMMARY COMPLETION

SUMMARY COMPLETION
  WITH A BOX

CLASSIFICATION

PICK FROM A LIST

Academic Reading Section 3

Section 1	13 questions	One passage	Approx 900 words
Section 2	13 questions	One passage	Approx 900 words
Section 3	**14 questions**	**One passage**	**Approx 900 words**

Question Types and Practice Tasks

PARAGRAPH HEADINGS

You choose the correct heading for each paragraph from a list of headings. There are always more headings than you need, so you will not need to use them all. You will never need to use a heading more than once. There may be some example headings too, so don't use these headings again.

The world's population is forecast to reach 7.5 billion by 2020, and growing prosperity, especially in China, is fuelling a rising appetite for meat and cereals. Yet it is becoming harder to find new farmland, water is increasingly scarce and crop-yield growth is slowing. Already 167 million children are malnourished. Are hungry times ahead?

What is a heading?

A heading covers the main idea of the paragraph.

1 Which of these three headings states the main idea in the paragraph on the left? Use the highlighted key words to help you decide.

  i Population figures for China
  ii Assessing China's farmland
  iii Global population and the future

2 How did the highlighted words help you?
3 How do the verb tenses help you find the answer?
4 Can you explain why the other headings are attractive, but wrong?

How should I write my answers?

You only need to write the correct number, i, ii, iii, etc. Don't waste time copying out the headings.

ACTION PLAN

▶ Read all the headings and underline or highlight the key words.
▶ Read the first paragraph of the passage, marking the topic sentence(s) and related phrases and vocabulary.
▶ Re-phrase the main idea of the paragraph in your mind.
▶ Read the list of headings to see if there is a match between the key words in the headings and the words you have marked in the paragraph.
▶ Choose the heading that best summarises the main idea of the first paragraph.
▶ Go on to the next paragraph and repeat the **Action Plan**.
▶ If you think two headings fit one paragraph, mark both of them and rule one of these out later.

NOW TRY THE TASK

*Choose the correct heading for paragraphs **A–C** from the list of headings below.*

List of Headings
i The destruction of the library
ii Collection methods
iii Replacing lost books
iv The library's original purpose
v Storage methods

5 Paragraph A
6 Paragraph B
7 Paragraph C

ℭ The old library of Alexandria ℭ

A The ancient library of Alexandria, which served as the intellectual and cultural hub of Egypt for 250 years, was tragically destroyed in 43 BC. Now there is widespread speculation about its true beginnings. The most popular theory is that Ptolemy I Soter (who ruled from 304 to 282 BC) gathered a vast selection of books on kingship, ruling and the world's people, so he might better understand trade terms and how to lead his subjects.

B Ptolemy I longed to possess all the literature in the world. The manuscripts took the form of scrolls kept in pigeonholes, the best of them wrapped in jackets of leather or linen. They are likely to have remained in the groups in which they were acquired, rather than being properly categorised. Parchment wasn't used until later, when the first books began to be written and kept in wooden chests in Roman times.

C As the library expanded, Ptolemy's successors used increasingly unscrupulous techniques to obtain manuscripts. One source claims that every ship sailing into Alexandria's harbour was routinely searched and, if a book was found, it was confiscated and taken to the library. There it was examined and a decision made whether to keep it and make a replacement copy, to be given to its rightful owner together with adequate reimbursement, or to just return the original copy outright.

8 Explain why the extra headings are attractive, but wrong.

SUMMARY COMPLETION

You complete the summary by writing no more than three words and/or a number from the passage in each gap. The summary may cover the ideas in the whole passage or may be based on a section of the passage only. You may be told which part it relates to. The answers may not be in passage order.

What is a summary completion question?

It is similar to sentence completion but here, you also need to pay attention to how the ideas are linked together.

9 Read the summary below and decide what type of information is missing. Look at the highlighted words to help you do this. What do the words *But this tiny* tell you about the type of answer needed in Question 10? Make a note of the type of word you predict for each answer.

10 ....

11 ....

12 ....

> Few people have ever heard of Yonaguni, in Japan's Okinawa island chain. But this tiny (10) .... has recently attracted international attention after the discovery of (11) .... Locals believe they are the remnants of a vast civilisation lost many years ago. The site is now a popular destination for (12) .... who like an underwater challenge.

How should I write my answers?

You should only use words from the passage, and you must use no more words than you are told to use. They should be written exactly as they are in the reading passage (numbers too) and they have to be spelt correctly. Do not include any unnecessary words, or repeat words that are already provided.

ACTION PLAN

▶ Read the instructions carefully to see how many words you can write, and whether you are told which paragraph(s) the summary comes from.

▶ Read the summary heading (if there is one) to help you find the right place in the passage.

▶ Read through the summary to get an idea of what it is about and how much of the passage it covers.

▶ Decide what kind of word is needed to complete the first gap, e.g. a noun, a name, an adjective.

▶ Note any grammatical clues, e.g. articles or prepositions, which may help you find the answer.

▶ Underline or highlight the key words around the gap.

▶ Read the passage quickly and decide where the answer to the first question comes from.

▶ Decide exactly which words or numbers you should write as your answer.

▶ Read above and below this part to find the rest of the answers.

NOW TRY THE TASK

Complete the summary below with words taken from the reading passage.
*Choose **ONE OR TWO WORDS AND/OR A NUMBER** for each answer.*

Gold bugs . . . .

Medieval alchemists found, in the end, that they could not create gold. Modern geochemists have a similar problem. They find it hard to understand how natural gold deposits form. There is much handwaving about gold-rich fluids from deep in the earth, and chemical precipitation, but the physics does not add up. The answer may be that what is happening is not geochemical at all, but biochemical. And a casual experiment conducted by a bacteriologist may hold the key.

Derek Lovley, of the University of Massachusetts, has been studying 'metal-eating' bacteria for two decades. These bacteria make their living by converting the dissolved ions of metallic elements from one electrical state to another. This reduction releases energy, which the bacteria extract for their own purposes.

Unsurprisingly, such bacteria tend to prefer common metals such as iron and manganese for lunch, though some species are able to subsist on such exotica as uranium. Dr Lovley decided to put some of his bacteria into a solution of gold chloride. He was fully prepared for nothing to happen, as gold compounds are generally toxic to bacteria. Instead, the test tube containing the solution turned a beautiful shade of purple, the colour of metallic gold when it is dispersed very finely in water.

☆ Creating gold ☆

Even today, scientists are unable to work out how gold is made. Recently, however, they have considered that the process may be (**13**) .... An experiment was carried out using bacteria that create their own (**14**) .... using metal. The types of metal these organisms usually feed on are either (**15**) .... or .... However, when the bacteria were added to a test tube of (**16**) .... solution, it changed (**17**) ...., indicating the presence of gold compounds.

18 Find words or phrases in the reading passage about gold bugs that have been replaced by the following words in the summary.

a are unable to work out	
b gold is made	
c the process	
d carried out	
e organisms	
f usually feed on	
g changed	

SUMMARY COMPLETION WITH A BOX

You complete the gaps in the summary by choosing the correct answer from a box of options. The options are usually single words but they may be short phrases. There will be some extra words in the box that you do not need to use. The summary may cover the ideas in the whole passage or may be based on a section of the passage only. You may be told which part it relates to.

How is this different from summary completion without a box?
You should follow the **Action Plan** on page 52, but you also need to match the ideas in the passage to the correct words in the box. This means that you will need to recognise synonyms or words that paraphrase ideas in the passage.

19 Look at the words *in italics* in B and underline or highlight the words in A that they have replaced.

A

Coral bleaching occurs when the important algae that live in corals become stressed and are expelled. This turns corals white, leaving them in an unhealthy state.

B

If *essential organisms* are *lost* from a coral reef, a process called coral bleaching can *take place*, which *renders* corals white and unhealthy.

20 What does *this*, in A, refer to?
21 What does *which*, in B, refer to?

How should I write my answers?
You only need to write the letters A, B, C, etc. Do not waste time copying out the words as well.

Key considerations

Research shows that, when choosing a home, most people are keen to find somewhere that is in the right place: that is close to work or study or has easy access to public transport. Property consultants agree that, cost aside, aspects such as the number or size of the rooms, or the furniture (if the property is furnished), play a secondary role.

In the same way, the medical care in hospitals and the hospital record on this are far more important to patients than things like whether the latest drugs are being used or whether the number of nurses and doctors is considered exemplary.

NOW TRY THE TASK

Read the passage on the left.
*Complete the summary using the list of words, **A–I**, below.*

Studies indicate that people generally focus on the **(22)** ...... of housing, rather than on the physical **(23)** ...... or the **(24)** ....

This general **(25)** ...... also applies to medical treatment. Patients note the quality of care, rather than focusing on the level of **(26)** ...... at the hospital.

A way	**F** location
B features	**G** principle
C contents	**H** prices
D staffing	**I** pieces
E movement	

27 Which words in the passage helped you choose the correct words from the box?

CLASSIFICATION

You decide which category some statements or features belong to. The categories are usually A, B, C, etc. The statements are usually numbered 1, 2, 3, etc. The answers are not in passage order.

What is classification?

In both classification and matching tasks, you have to match things together. However, in classification you may have *both/all* and *neither/nor* options.

Imagine you are choosing between two jobs – Job A and Job B – and there are certain conditions that you are looking for. You could write down the conditions as statements and then match them to the jobs on offer.

1 pays more than $100 per day
2 offers more than 30 days annual leave
3 operates a flexitime system

Job A

Earn $150 plus a day, five days a week, in this fast-paced advertising company. If you're prepared to do long hours for a good salary, call now.

Job B

Fed up with working late and getting no time off? Join Pelly's and Co. and get 40 days holiday a year plus an income in excess of $120 a day.

Condition 1 is true of both jobs, condition 2 is true of Job B and condition 3 is true of neither job. This is a way of classifying the conditions.

How should I write my answers?

You only need to write the correct letter (A, B, C, etc.).

ACTION PLAN

▶ Underline or highlight the categories in the passage. These are often names, dates or nouns. Sometimes they are close together in the passage; sometimes they are found across the whole passage.
▶ Underline or highlight the key words in the statements.
▶ Read around each category in the passage and re-read the statements. Check whether any (or none) of the language in the passage relates to the ideas in the statements. Then decide which category is correct for each statement.
▶ If you have *both* and/or *neither* categories, you need to check the information in the passage for these, too.

NOW TRY THE TASK

Classify the following features as being true of

A Relief
B Calm
C Both Relief and Calm
D Neither Relief nor Calm

28 is suitable for children
29 causes sleepiness
30 is easy to swallow
31 works quickly

What's the difference?

Two products, *Relief* and *Calm*, both claim to get rid of a headache in a short period of time, but while *Relief* is a homeopathic form of medication that has been developed using natural substances, *Calm* is a more conventional product that contains a range of chemicals, some of which may be harmful if taken in large quantities. Doctors also advise that these chemicals may interfere with certain activities, such as driving, and should be avoided if the patient needs to stay awake. *Relief*, it seems, causes no such problems.

It is no wonder that parents are keen to find alternatives for their children to drugs containing chemicals, but are products like *Relief* the answer? Surprisingly not, according to the product label, which, like that of its more conventional counterpart, warns against giving the medicine to anyone under the age of fourteen. Both medicines come in tablet form – making them less easy to digest than soluble products. However, the years of research seem to have paid off for *Calm*, which is now little bigger than a pinhead, while the bullet-sized *Relief* might prove a bit more troublesome.

32 Check your answers to questions 28–31 by putting a ✓ or ✗ in the boxes below under each type of medicine and write the letter A, B, C or D as the answer.

Features	Relief	Calm	Answer
28 is suitable for children	✗	✗	D
29 causes sleepiness			
30 is easy to swallow			
31 works quickly			

PICK FROM A LIST

You pick the correct answers from a list of options. There are usually two or three answers to pick from about six options, but there may be more. The options are labelled A, B, C, etc. The answers may not be in passage order.

How is this question different from multiple choice?

In multiple choice you only pick one correct answer, and the answers to each question are in one small area of the passage. In pick from a list you pick a number of answers (usually two or three) from a list of five or six options and you may need to read a larger area of the passage.

How should I write my answers?

You only need to write the correct letter (A, B, C, etc.). You can write these in any order. Sometimes a question is worth one mark (for finding all the answers) and sometimes the question is worth one mark for each correct answer, so be careful how you fill out your answer sheet.

ACTION PLAN

▶ Read the question carefully and note how many options you must pick and how many marks they are worth.
▶ Underline or highlight the key words in the question and options.
▶ Read the passage and find words or expressions that match the options.
▶ Check that the options you choose mean the same as in the passage.

NOW TRY THE TASK

Questions 33 and 34
Choose TWO letters A–F.
*Which **TWO** facts about chewing gum are mentioned by the writer?*

A how it is produced
B the variety of tastes it produces
C where it is most commonly manufactured
D how the consumer market has changed
E the fact that it can protect teeth
F when it is best to chew it

Chewing gum is not considered a sophisticated pursuit. Munching on mastic-tree sap was one of the less admirable habits of the ancient Greeks. The sight of people masticating open-mouthed on today's synthetic latex gum, together with sticky encounters under seats, explains why such enlightened places as Singapore banned the anti-social stuff. Yet chewing gum has, quietly, come of age. No longer just for kids to blow bubbles with, it is becoming popular among adults: to fight cavities, cure ear infections and soothe an ulcer. And the evolution of chewing gum from a sticky-sweet vice into a 'nutraceutical' – the fashionable term for foods with medicinal properties – is driving sales.

35 Which phrases in the passage match the two answers?

ANSWERS PAGE 110
PRACTICE TEST PAGE 101

The Academic Writing Test

A 60-minute test of your ability to write in English

How many parts does the writing test have?
There are two tasks but Task 2 is worth more marks than Task 1, so it is important to try to keep to the recommended timing for each part.

Task 1 (about 20 minutes)
You write a 150-word summary of the information provided in a graph, chart, table or diagram, or a combination of these.

Task 2 (about 40 minutes)
You write a discursive essay of 250 words in response to a question or argument on a general topic.

What is the writing test like?
You will receive a question paper with two writing tasks on it and an answer sheet. The tasks are not related in any way and require quite different answers. You must write your answers to both tasks within the hour.

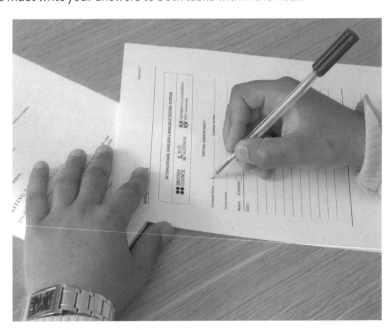

Is there any choice of tasks?
No. You have to do the two tasks you are given.

Why are there two tasks in the writing test?
It is important that the examiner can see how good you are at different types of writing. You have to show how well you can summarise factual information. You also have to demonstrate your ability to write a clear, well-structured argument.

How is the writing test marked?
The writing test is marked using a 9-band scale, like all other parts of the test. The examiner will be looking at four features of your written language: **content**, **organisation**, **vocabulary** and **grammar**.

☐ ON THE DAY

- The writing test is the third part of the IELTS test. It takes place after the reading test on the same day.

- You receive a question paper and an answer sheet that has enough space to write your answer for both tasks.

- You can write in pencil or pen.

- You cannot use rough paper but you can write on the question paper.

- If you make any notes on the answer sheet, cross them out before you hand it in.

- You can ask the administrator for an extra answer sheet if you need it.

- Make sure you write the answer to each task in the correct section of the booklet.

- You will get time checks after 20 minutes and just before the end of the whole test.

- You must stop writing after one hour or you may be disqualified.

- You cannot leave the room until the test is over.

Content	Is the **content** of your answer accurate, relevant and appropriate?
Task 1	Is there a general overview of the information? Have you selected key features to describe? Have you used the information to illustrate the points?
Task 2	Have you made your position clear? Are the main ideas clear? Are the ideas well supported? Is there a relevant conclusion?
Organisation	Is the **organisation** of your answer clear and logical? Is the development of the whole answer logical? Have you used paragraphs appropriately? Are the sentences well linked to each other? Are the links between ideas clear?

Vocabulary	Is your choice of **vocabulary** appropriate and have you used words accurately? Have you used a range of appropriate words and expressions? Have you used some idiomatic or less common expressions? Have you avoided repeating the same words? Have you used words in their correct form? Is your spelling accurate?
Grammar	Is your choice of sentences and structures varied and is your **grammar** accurate? Have you used complex and simple sentences? Have you used a range of accurate structures? Can the examiner understand what you mean? Is your punctuation accurate?

What if I don't understand the tasks?

You cannot ask the administrator any questions about the tasks. If you do not understand, you should at least write something based on the task and topic. By doing this, you will lose fewer marks, because answers that are on a different topic, or that are memorised, lose a lot of marks.

What general approach should I take to the writing test?

As there are two tasks in the writing test, timing is very important. You must make sure you leave enough time to complete Task 2 because it is worth more marks than Task 1.

You must answer the questions you are asked. For Task 1, don't give opinions on the diagram, just summarise the information following the guidelines given. For Task 2, read the question carefully and then write your answer on the topic, making sure you support all your points. Leave time at the end of the test to read through your answers and check for mistakes.

Can I write in note form?

No. You should write complete sentences for both tasks and organise your answers into clear paragraphs. Answers that are written as notes lose marks and you cannot get a high mark for organisation if you do not use paragraphs.

Can I write in capital letters?

You should avoid writing in capital letters because the examiner needs to know whether you can punctuate your work and use capital letters correctly.

What if I write under or over the word limits?

You should try to keep to the word limits. If you write too few words, you will lose marks. There are no extra marks for writing more, so if you have time to spare, use this to check through what you have written, rather than writing extra.

How can I improve my score in the writing test?

You can help to improve your score by making sure that you know what types of writing you will be expected to do and what the examiner will be looking for. The following pages, divided into Task 1 and Task 2, cover these points thoroughly and provide you with an **Action Plan** for each task.

Academic Writing Task 1

Task 1	150 words	20 minutes	Summary information
Task 2	250 words	40 minutes	Discursive essay

What do I have to do in Task 1?
You have to describe in 150 words the information provided in a graph, chart, table or diagram. There may be more than one of these in the task.

What if I have difficulty reading graphs and charts?
You will need to practise this skill to be able to do this task. Graphs and charts communicate information visually. Knowing how they work will help you to summarise the data.

What sort of graphs or diagrams could I get?
You could get any of the following, or a variation on these formats.

Pie chart

Line graph

Bar graph

	Year	Name	Description
1			
2			
3			

Table

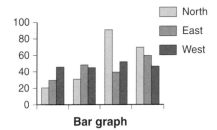

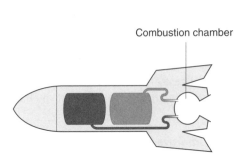

Combustion chamber

Diagram of how something works

Diagram of a process

Look at the chart, the graphs and the table on the previous page and then complete the summary below using words from the box.

Pie charts are used to show parts of a whole and to represent these at a set point in time. They do not show variations in the data over time. However, each of the parts may be shown as a (**1**) ....

Line graphs can be used to show how something (**2**) .... over time. They have an x-axis (horizontal) and a y-axis ((**3**) ....). Usually the x-axis has numbers for the (**4**) .... period and the y-axis has numbers for what is being measured. Line graphs can be used when you are plotting (**5**) .... that have peaks (ups) and (**6**) .... (downs). In other words, they can show (**7**) ....

Bar graphs are similar to (**8**) .... graphs in that they have two (**9**) .... and are useful when you want to show how something has changed over the (**10**) .... (or days or weeks), especially where there are really big changes. They are also very useful if you want to (**11**) .... things by showing their differences or similarities.

Tables contain words, numbers or signs, or a combination of these, displayed in (**12**) .... or boxes to illustrate a set of facts and the relationship between them.

line	axes	percentage
columns	vertical	trends
time	troughs	data
compare	years	changes

▶▶▶▶▶▶▶▶▶▶▶▶▶▶▶▶▶▶

CONTENT

You must summarise the information in your own words, highlighting the key features and supporting these with the figures or information given. You should also make comparisons where appropriate, and provide an overview. Your answer should be in the correct format, i.e. a continuous piece of writing. You should not explain or give an opinion on the information.

What should I do first?

You should analyse the task carefully before you start to write. Read the heading(s) and note any labels or words. For bar and line graphs, look at the x- and y-axes to understand what they mean. For diagrams, note the process or sequence of events and any other information that is supplied. Try to form an overview in your mind of the information that is provided.

How should I begin my answer?

Write an introduction in your own words, describing the information. You can use individual words from the question paper, but if you copy long phrases or whole sentences, these words will be deducted from the total word count of your answer.

Look at this bar graph and complete the introduction below.

Graph 1

Sports played by children between 5 & 14 years old in Australia in 2003

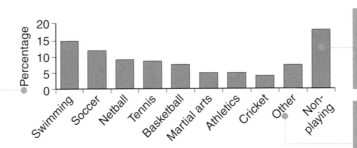

Bar values do not total 100% because some children will play more than one sport.

Highest individual value shown, but these are people who do not play a sport.

x-axis shows *Other* = sports not specifically identified by name.

> The bar graph shows the **(1)** .... sports that are enjoyed by young children in Australia in 2003, and compares their popularity by showing the **(2)** .... of children involved in each sport.

What are key features?

Key features are the most noticeable, significant facts contained in the graph. You should select at least three key features, which will form the basis of your answer. Do not try to mention everything.

Look at the graph again and complete this list of key features.

- Most popular sports: swimming and **(3)** .... : mention %
- 'Non-playing' category significant: mention %
- Least popular sport: **(4)** ....

How do I support the key features with data?

You cannot include all the data in your answer, so you need to select the most interesting data related to the key features to illustrate your summary.

Complete the paragraph below with features and data taken from the graph.

> According to the graph, the most popular sport among 5–14-year-olds is **(5)** .... , closely followed by **(6)** .... In fact, **(7)** .... of children go swimming and a slightly smaller percentage play soccer. The largest **(8)** .... involves 18% of children, who do not play any sports at all. The least popular activity is **(9)** .... , which is played by only **(10)** .... of children.

What is an overview?

An overview is usually one or two sentences summarising the general trends or information given in the graph, chart or diagram. The overview can come at the beginning, in the middle or at the end of your summary. It often forms a useful conclusion.

Complete the overview below for the information in Graph 1 on the previous page.

> Some of the sports played by Australian children are more (**11**) .... than others and, while not all young children are involved in sport, the (**12**) .... of them are.

What if I get a diagram?

You may get a diagram showing how something works or illustrating a process or sequence of events. You should follow the same procedure as you would for a graph or chart.

Look at the diagram below. Write an introduction (one sentence) in your own words and then complete the first part of the answer below, which provides an overview, selects some key features and supports these with data.

Glass making

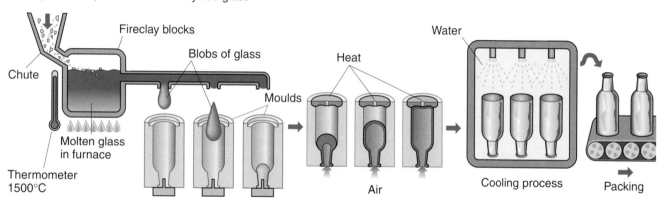

> **Your introduction here**
>
> (**13**) ....
>
> ....
>
> The process involves a number of stages, during which the glass undergoes various forms of treatment, before the final product is manufactured.
>
> The raw materials that go into making glass include sand, soda ash and limestone. First, these are sent down a chute into a furnace, along with (**14**) .... The furnace is made of fireclay blocks and (**15**) .... the raw materials to a temperature of 1500 degrees centigrade until (**16**) .... is formed.

How do I compare data?

Some graphs or charts contain more than one set of data. For example, Graph 2 below compares the participation of boys and girls in different sports.

Use the words in the box to complete these sentences, which compare some of the data.

most popular
while
fewer
hardly
more

17 .... boys than girls play soccer.

18 The .... sport among girls is netball.

19 .... swimming is popular among boys and girls, ... boys participate in this sport.

20 ...... any girls play cricket.

21 Now describe the graph in at least two paragraphs. Write an introductory sentence about the purpose of this graph. Select three key features to include in your description and decide which data to use to illustrate them. Make some comparisons and provide a general overview.

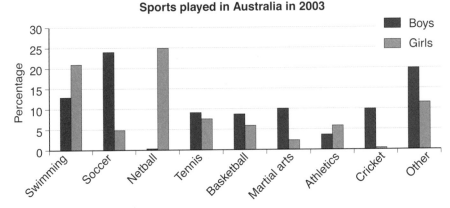

Sports played in Australia in 2003

What if I get more than one graph?

It is quite common for Task 1 to involve more than once piece of information relating to the topic. In this case, you will have to describe and compare the information.

22 In the table below, list the similarities and differences between the graph above and the graph on page 62. Decide what three key features you would choose to include in a comparison of the two sets of data. They may not be what you chose first when you had only one chart to deal with.

Similarities	Differences	Key features
Both deal with children's sport in Australia		

Complete the introduction and first paragraph below of an answer based on a comparison of the two graphs.

The first graph shows which sports are most popular among Australian children, and the second graph compares boys' and girls' (**23**) .... in these activities.

The first graph shows that (**24**) .... is the most popular sport among Australian children, with 15% of children participating. However, from the second graph we can see that there are almost twice as many (**25**) .... involved in this sport as (**26**) .... By contrast, while 12% of all children play soccer, the (**27**) .... of boys playing this sport is far greater than that for girls, with only 5% of girls playing soccer compared to almost 25% of boys.

28 Complete the answer by adding another paragraph and providing an overview of the information.

ORGANISATION

You must present the information and ideas in a clear, logical manner, using linking words and paragraphs appropriately.

How many paragraphs do I write?

There is no rule about how many paragraphs there should be in a Task 1 answer, but each paragraph should introduce a new main idea. For example, you could write an introductory paragraph and two or three others, and conclude with an overview.

Look at Graph 3 below. Using the box to help you, decide what to include in your answer.

Graph 3

Introduction
how much people eat

Key features

1 ....

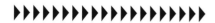

2 ....

3 ....

Concluding paragraph with overview

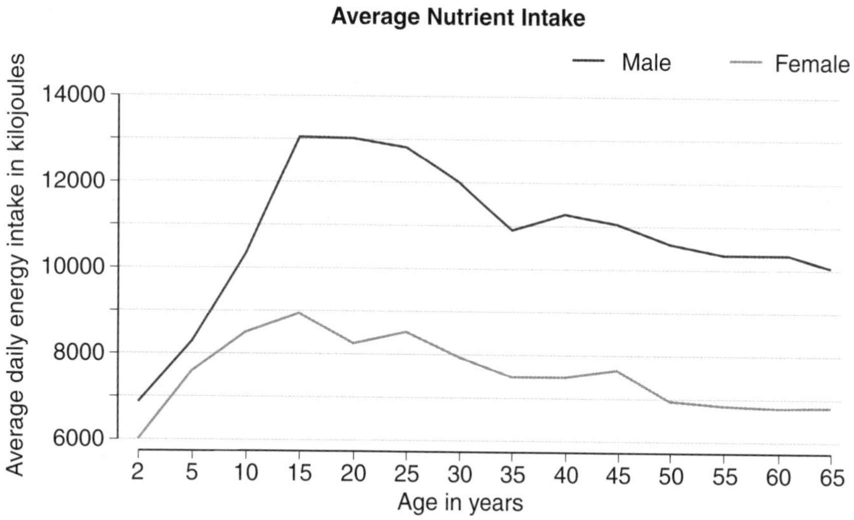
Average Nutrient Intake
Male
Female
Average daily energy intake in kilojoules
14000
12000
10000
8000
6000
2
5
10
15
20
25
30
35
40
45
50
55
60
65
Age in years

Decide how many paragraphs you will need for the key features, and what information to include in each. Complete these ideas in your own words.

> The graph shows how many kilojoules people consume, on average, between the (**4**) .... and compares the figures for men and women.
>
> The overall trend for males and females is (**5**) .... However, males consume (**6**) .... throughout their lives, and at the age of 15, they eat a grand total of (**7**) .... The intake of females is also (**8**) .... at this age, although their (**9**) .... of consumption is much lower, being just under (**10**) ....

How can I link my ideas?

You can link your ideas by using words or phrases such as *similarly* and *however*. It is also sometimes useful to connect the new paragraph to the previous one using a structure such as *As far as ... is/are concerned*.

Complete this paragraph which continues the description of the graph on page 65. Choose appropriate linkers from the box.

in the case of
if
as
also
with
furthermore
generally
after this
as far as ..... are concerned

> (**11**) .... , most people eat between six and seven thousand kilojoules in their early years, and this figure rises quite steeply (**12**) .... they move into their teens. (**13**) .... , food intake tends to decline, (**14**) .... both age groups eating less as they get older. The difference in the amounts eaten in later years (**15**) .... narrows to around three thousand kilojoules. Thus it is (**16**) .... clear that we need more food when we are young and less when we are old.

Another way to link your ideas within a paragraph is to use a reference word that incorporates the meaning of the original word, such as *the, this, these, neither, both, one, it, who, whom,* etc.

Find a word or phrase to complete the gaps. There may be more than one possibility.

17 Though food intake increases as young women get older, ... falls after the age of 15.

18 At the age of two, young boys eat about 7000 kilojoules per day. .... increases significantly up to the age of 15.

19 Men and women eat a lot when they are under 20, but .... eat less after .... age.

20 While men eat more than women, ... groups follow a similar pattern of food intake.

21 Food consumption varies between men and women, with .... difference occurring at the age of 15.

22 By the age of 50, females only consume 7000 kilojoules, ... is considerably less than men.

How can I make sure my vocabulary is appropriate?
You need to be precise in your choice of words.

Look at the words in italics in the paragraph below. Replace them with more suitable words to improve the paragraph.

Graph 4

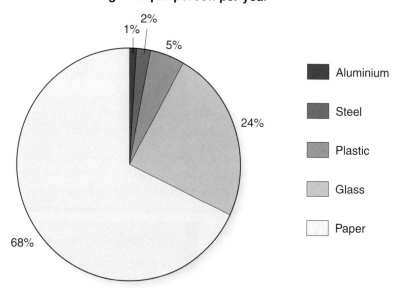

Recycling in Sydney
91 kilograms per person per year

- Aluminium
- Steel
- Plastic
- Glass
- Paper

The pie chart shows the amount of **(1)** *stuff* which is recycled in Australia by each person **(2)** *each year*. It is **(3)** *known* from the **(4)** *table* that the most **(5)** *usually* recycled material is paper, **(6)** *and the following* is glass. Aluminium makes up only 1% of the **(7)** *whole*.

What else can I do to improve my vocabulary score?
You also need to know which words collocate or go together well.

8 Match the adjectives in box A with the nouns in box B to make collocations. There may be more than one possibility.

A

vast   serious   small
downward   considerable   reasonable

B

trend   number   majority   minority
consideration   proportion   amount

How can I show a range of vocabulary?

You should find different ways of expressing similar ideas. Try to avoid repeating the same words or using vague words.

Match words and phrases 9–16 to the words and phrases with a similar meaning a–h.

9 few   **a** the majority of
10 less than   **b** a marked increase
11 a steep rise   **c** the most significant
12 fell dramatically   **d** a small number of
13 compares   **e** provides a comparison of
14 most   **f** overall
15 generally speaking   **g** under
16 the biggest   **h** dropped considerably

How important is accuracy?

You need to pay attention to how you choose, form and spell words. You will lose marks if you make mistakes in these areas.

17 Correct the errors in spelling and word choice in this short paragraph.

These days, every Sydney residents recycles an average of 91 kilograms of waste each year. This includes a hole range of different materials, from paper to steel and aluminum.

Overall, 68 per cent of the recycling waste is paper. In fact, the paper figure is higher than that of all the other producers put together. The next highest figure is that for glass – 24 per cent of glass is normal recycled, while only very small quantitys of plastic and other types of waste are recycled.

▶▶▶▶▶▶▶▶▶▶▶▶▶▶▶▶▶▶▶▶▶

GRAMMAR

You need to show that you can use a range of structures and that you can use grammar accurately. You also need to punctuate your writing well.

How can I show a range of structures?

You should show that you can handle different tenses and verb phrases.

Here is a description of a diagram of a waterfall. Put the verbs in the correct form.

The diagram shows how water (**1**) *can / pump* from a pond to create an ornamental waterfall.

For this to work, the pond (**2**) *need / situate* near a wall. Above the pond is a basin, about 25 centimetres deep, which (**3**) *act* as a reservoir for the waterfall. This (**4**) *sink* into the rock or wall, approximately three metres above the pond. Water (**5**) *pump* up to the basin from the pond.

When the basin is full, it (**6**) *overflow*, creating a stream of water. To maintain this constant flow, a 32-volt pump (**7**) *use / carry* the water up. The pump (**8**) *submerge* in the pond and (**9**) *connect* to a transformer by a cable. A narrow pipe (**10**) *attach* to the pump and (**11**) *carry* the water up to the basin. The pipe (**12**) *conceal* in the wall so that it (**13**) *appear* as if the water (**14**) *flow* naturally rather than (**15**) *recycle* from the pond. Thus a simple system using a pump and a small pool results in a continuous fall of water.

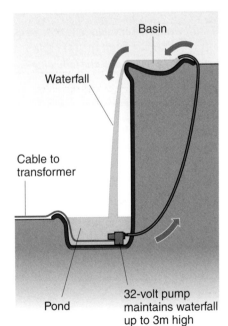

Basin
Waterfall
Cable to transformer
Pond
32-volt pump maintains waterfall up to 3m high

How important is grammatical accuracy?

You will lose marks if you make grammatical errors in your writing, particularly when errors are frequent and affect meaning.

Look at the table below. Read the first two paragraphs of the sample answer and make the changes suggested in the box to improve them. Then complete the answer by finishing the third and fourth paragraphs.

Chocolate consumption – kilos per head in 2002

Country	Kilos per head (female)	Kilos per head (male)	Total kilos per head
Brazil	0.5	0.4	0.9
Japan	0.8	1.0	1.8
Australia	2.2	2.2	4.4
Belgium	4.0	2.8	6.8
UK	4.0	4.4	8.4
Austria	6.0	3.8	9.8
Switzerland	5.0	5.3	10.3

16 Use a different verb in a passive form.
17 Correct the verb form.
18 Correct the verb form or change the sentence structure.
19 Use the correct superlative form.
20 Correct the verb form.
21 Correct the article.
22 Correct the tense.

The table provides information on how much chocolate (**16**) *people ate* in a range of different countries around the world. It (**17**) *show* the number of kilos per head (**18**) *was eaten* in 2002 and provides a breakdown of these figures for men and women.

Total chocolate consumption ranges from 0.9 to 10.3 kilos per head. The country with the (**19**) *higher* consumption of chocolate is Switzerland, where an average of 10.3 kilos (**20**) *consumed* per person. In Austria we see (**21**) *the* very similar consumption pattern. By contrast, Brazilians (**22**) *would eat* the least amount of chocolate.

As far as consumption for men and women is concerned, ...

Overall it seems that ....

ACTION PLAN

▶ Read the task and decide what type of graph, chart, table or diagram it is.
▶ Read the heading and note any labels or words.
▶ Decide what the important information is and note down some data.
▶ Write an opening sentence or paragraph.
▶ Write two or three more paragraphs based on the key information.
▶ Illustrate this with some supporting material.
▶ Try to use a range of relevant vocabulary and sentence types.
▶ Make sure you have included an overview.
▶ Finish your answer with an appropriate concluding sentence.
▶ Leave time to check your answer for errors. Look at spelling, grammar and punctuation.
▶ Count the number of words you have used.

☛ **ANSWERS PAGE 111**
PRACTICE TEST PAGE 104

Academic Writing Task 2

Task 1	150 words	20 minutes	Summary of information
Task 2	**250 words**	**40 minutes**	**Discursive essay**

What do I have to do in Task 2?

Task 2 is a topic on which you have to write a discursive essay. The topic may be in the form of a statement or a question. Sometimes different or opposing views are expressed; sometimes there is one view to discuss.

▶▶▶▶▶▶▶▶▶▶▶▶▶▶▶▶▶▶

CONTENT

You must answer all parts of the task. You need to make your own position clear and provide main ideas and supporting arguments to illustrate this. You should write a clear introduction and conclusion.

How can I make sure I answer all parts of the task?

You should analyse the task carefully so that you know exactly what you have to write about.

Look at the notes on task A and the summary of these in the table below.

A

These are opposing views.

such as tells me that these are examples – I can discuss other things if I want to.

Some people think that teenagers' use of the internet should be limited. Others feel that the internet is an academic resource that they should have free access to, in order to do things such as homework and projects.

Discuss both these views and give your opinion.

I must discuss both views – so it would help to think about who would have these different views and why.

I must say what I think.

Task	Are opposing views expressed?	What are the key words?	How many parts must I write about?
A	Yes	*teenagers / internet / limited / academic resource*	*Two – limiting or not limiting internet use*
B			
C			

1 Read these tasks and then complete the table on page 70.

B

Some parents believe that extra private lessons outside school hours, where students work alone with a teacher, can help them do better at school. Others disagree.

What are the advantages and disadvantages of private tuition?

C

Traffic congestion seems to be increasing.

What do you think are the causes of traffic congestion and what, if anything, can be done to reduce the problems?

What is my 'position'?
Your position is your view on the topic. Make sure that you say what your position is, and that it stays the same, i.e. you don't contradict yourself.

Look at task B above. What is your position?
  i Private tuition has more advantages than disadvantages.
 ii Private tuition has more disadvantages than advantages.
iii The advantages and disadvantages of private tuition are fairly equal.

2 How is task C different from B? What is your position likely to be?

How do I make my position clear?
You should state your position clearly, perhaps as part of your introduction, support it throughout your answer and re-state it (in a different way) in the conclusion.

3 Underline or highlight the writer's position in this introduction to task B. Is it position i, ii or iii?

> In many countries students have to compete to get into colleges and universities when they leave school. For this reason, some parents decide to pay for extra lessons to help their children be more successful. On the whole, I feel that this is a good idea, despite some of the drawbacks of private tuition.

4 Change the last sentence so that the paragraph expresses position ii.
5 You need to re-state your position in the conclusion, by pulling together your main ideas and showing how they support your argument. Underline or highlight the writer's position in this conclusion.

> Evidently private tuition is something that has to be considered carefully. However, there is no doubt that it can be enormously helpful in preparing students for important examinations by giving them the extra help they need. Overall, these benefits outweigh the disadvantages.

6 Write your own introduction to task B.

What is a main idea?

A main idea is a key point or argument that relates directly to the question and to your position. You only need a few main ideas, but remember that you may need main ideas on both sides of an argument.

7 Complete these notes, which give some main ideas for task B on page 71.

ADVANTAGES	DISADVANTAGES
Lessons go at student's .... of learning	Cost ....
Student can ask more	Students are already very ....
More attention on	Time needed to travel to ....

What if I don't have any ideas?

If you cannot think of your own ideas, think about what you have read on the topic in books or magazines, or seen on television.

How do I make my main ideas clear?

Your main ideas should come between the introduction and conclusion, and form the body of your answer. Each main idea should be in a separate paragraph.

What are supporting arguments?

Supporting arguments add extra information to your main ideas. You should link the main idea to the topic and then support it.

8 Underline or highlight the sentence which contains the supporting argument in this paragraph from task B on page 71.

One of the reasons why private tuition leads to better exam results is the fact that the tutor can teach at the student's own pace. This is not possible in a classroom with a lot of students because there, the teacher has to go at an average pace to suit everyone.

9 Note some main ideas for task C on page 71, using these headings.

Causes of congestion	How to reduce problems
....	....
....	....
....	....

10 Look again at task C on page 71. Write an introductory paragraph, and another that includes a main idea and supporting arguments.

ORGANISATION
Your answer needs to develop logically from your introduction through several paragraphs to your conclusion. Within the paragraphs, your ideas should be linked together well.

How do I decide how many paragraphs to write?
Write between five and seven paragraphs: your introductory paragraph, three to five paragraphs for the main body of your answer, and your concluding paragraph. Aim to have one main idea in each paragraph.

1 This long paragraph would be better if it was broken into two paragraphs. Where could you start the second paragraph? To help you, underline or highlight the two sentences which contain the main ideas.

> Private tuition can result in more successful learning for a number of reasons. The most significant of these is the fact that a personal tutor is able to teach individual students at their own pace. A class teacher, on the other hand, has to keep everyone involved in the lesson. This means choosing a pace that suits the 'average' student but may not suit many individual students. Students can get more personal attention when they are taught on their own. They do not have to worry about understanding something straight away, as it can be repeated as many times as necessary and they can ask lots of questions. This is often not practical in a classroom situation because other students may get bored and, as a result, become disruptive.

How can I develop my answer logically?
You need to start each new paragraph with a word or phrase that shows that you are making a new or related point, e.g. *While this is a popular view; Not everyone takes such an approach; Another possible cause; As far as X is concerned.* You should do this to make your ideas clear.

2 Which of the following expressions could you use to begin your second paragraph above, so that it links well to the first paragraph?
  i Nevertheless, some people feel that
  ii It is also the case that
  iii Initially
  iv However

3 Why are the other three expressions not appropriate?

4 Complete the paragraph openers below for the task on traffic congestion (task C on page 71). Avoid using the words *first*, *second* or *third*.

There are a number of ways that we can help solve the problems of traffic congestion.

Paragraph 1 .... would be to make sure that every family only has one car.

Paragraph 2 .... would be to increase the cost of petrol.

Paragraph 3 A .... solution would be to charge people for road use.

How can I link my ideas within paragraphs?

You can link your ideas by using linking words and phrases, e.g. *however, yet, unfortunately, indeed, then* or *generally speaking*. Note that they don't always have to be at the start of a sentence.

5 Here are some supporting points for the three paragraphs about traffic congestion. Add each point to the right paragraph by using the words given to link up the ideas.

> Although seems difficult, can share / use public transport

> If more expensive / people will drive less / walk / take a bus / as a result less traffic

> Generally speaking, approach successful / particularly very busy roads

6 Read task D, then look at the introductory paragraph in which the reference words have been highlighted. Complete the table showing what they refer to.

D

Water is an increasingly valuable resource, but people continue to waste a lot of it. Some governments want to impose permanent water restrictions on domestic and agricultural use. Others feel we should put more effort into recycling water.

To what extent do you agree with these two solutions?

Water is definitely an invaluable resource. Without **it**, we cannot survive. Today many governments recognise that **they** need to limit the water that **their** citizens use. **Some** also attempt to recycle water. **Both approaches** to water conservation are necessary and should be promoted, though I feel **the first** is generally more successful.

it	water	some	
they		both approaches	
their		the first	

7 Complete the gaps in the two paragraphs below with a correct reference word from the box. Some of the words will be used more than once.

which
their
these
they
this
the
where

In countries (a) .... water seems to be readily available, people may, at first, be reluctant to reduce (b) .... water consumption. So initially, governments need to make (c) .... citizens aware of the consequences of using too much of (d) .... valuable resource. Once people realise that water supplies are limited and that (e) .... have a responsibility for conserving water, (f) .... task will be easier.

It must be remembered that people use water for many different purposes, (g) .... range from running domestic appliances such as washing machines to large-scale agricultural projects that need large quantities of water for irrigation. In (h) .... efforts to reduce water use, governments need to target all (i) .... different types of water consumption. (j) .... will often involve creating special laws.

8 Underline or highlight the other linking words in these two paragraphs.

9 Write a third paragraph about recycling water. Include one main idea and some supporting arguments, and link your ideas together well.

▶▶▶▶▶▶▶▶▶▶▶▶▶▶▶▶▶▶

VOCABULARY

You need to show that you have a range of vocabulary related to the topic and that you can use these words appropriately and accurately in your answer.

How can I improve my vocabulary range?
You have to know enough words to be accurate and avoid repetition. You can improve your vocabulary related to different topics by reading newspaper and magazine articles and noting some of the topic vocabulary.

1 Read the extract below, in which the vocabulary related to task C on page 71 has been highlighted. What sort of publication do you think it comes from?

CLUNK, CLICK, VROOM – AND AWAY WE GO. Every day, millions of us climb into our cars and set off on journeys to work, to the shops or just to enjoy ourselves. And once inside our cars, few of us are inclined to spare a thought for the environmental impact of driving in heavy traffic. Advertising consistently portrays cars as symbols of personal status and freedom, and sources of comfort and convenience.

But behind the shiny commercials, the costs of our car-dependent lifestyles are becoming increasingly serious. The lengthening traffic jams, demands for new roads, increasing air pollution and threat of climate change are all issues we must tackle sooner rather than later.

Emissions from different forms of transport are the fastest-growing source of greenhouse-gas pollution – mainly in the form of CO_2 arising from the combustion of diesel and petrol.

2 Complete these paragraphs for task C, using the highlighted words or phrases in the extract on page 75.

Most people would agree that traffic problems are increasing worldwide. In many large cities, it is hard to drive freely because traffic jams are so common. As a result, (a) .... is now a serious problem in cities because so much (b) .... is being used, and the issue of (c) .... has been directly linked to the human need for fast methods of (d) .... Why has this happened?

Initially, cars were a practical way of getting from A to B. They were not built to travel at high speeds and dual carriageways were unknown. If their (e) .... were relatively short, people often chose to walk, rather than drive. At this time, governments responded to complaints about (f) .... congestion by building (g) .... , unaware of the (h) .... this might have on the environment.

Nowadays, cars have become (i) .... – everyone wants one and it's hard to stop this because of their (j) .... and .... Unfortunately, we have become used to our (k) .... and we are reluctant to change.

How can I improve my accuracy?
You need to pay attention to how you choose, form and spell words. You will lose marks if you make mistakes in these areas.

3 Complete the gaps in these paragraphs with the correct form of the words in the box.

| crowd |
| special |
| drive |
| delay |
| |
| waste |
| |
| few |
| |
| |
| increase |
| manufacture |
| expense |
| charge |

Beijing is a very crowded city and traffic jams are common, (a) .... at peak travel times. Between six and seven in the evening, (b) .... know that the traffic will be bad and that they will have to expect (c) .... on their journeys. Everyone has got used to this, although no-one likes (d) .... time stuck in traffic.

In the past, there were far (e) .... cars in Beijing because they were too expensive to buy, but nowadays an (f) .... number of citizens can afford one because the car (g) .... industry in China is booming. In addition to this, petrol is relatively (h) .... compared to the prices (i) .... in many other countries.

▶▶▶▶▶▶▶▶▶▶▶▶▶▶▶▶▶

GRAMMAR
You need to show that you can write a range of sentence types and that you can use grammar accurately. You also need to punctuate your writing well.

How can I show a range of sentence types?
You should include both simple and complex sentences in your essay. (Complex sentences contain more than one clause.)

Look at this paragraph from a student's essay. The sentences are all simple, so the examiner cannot give a high mark for grammar, even though the meaning is clear.

Nearly all countries have traffic problems. They can be hard to solve. Local people can reduce some of the problems. They can choose to walk rather than drive. But this is often not a popular option. So the number of vehicles on the roads rises. However, sometimes there are poor road or traffic conditions. There is not much the public can do about this. Governments must take steps to reduce congestion. This means imposing laws.

Here is the same paragraph, re-written with a wider range of sentence types. This will get a better mark.

Nearly all countries have traffic problems, which can be hard to solve. Local people can reduce some of the problems by choosing to walk rather than drive, but this is often not a popular option. So the number of vehicles on the roads rises. If there are poor roads or traffic conditions, however, there is not much the public can do. Either way, governments clearly need to take steps to reduce congestion and this may mean imposing laws.

How can I improve my accuracy?

As well as checking for grammar mistakes, you should also make sure your punctuation is accurate.

1 Find the punctuation errors in this paragraph (there is one on each line).

commas needed round *unlike bicycles*
a ....
b ....
c ....
d ....
e ....
f ....
g ....

It is a well-known fact that cars and buses unlike bicycles use lots of petrol and create a great deal of pollution, surely something can be done about this. If we cannot get people to walk or, share vehicles we should put more pressure on scientist's to build solar powered engines. Although it may take some time to achieve this, it would be worth it? There are other alternatives, too. For example: if we all started driving electric cars, the world would be a much cleaner place

ACTION PLAN

▶ Analyse the task to see how many parts you have to write about.
▶ Decide on your position and your main ideas.
▶ Introduce your answer by re-phrasing the question and stating your position.
▶ Write three to five paragraphs on your main ideas, with supporting arguments.
▶ Link your ideas together so that your answer is logical and clearly developed.
▶ Try to use a range of relevant vocabulary and sentence types.
▶ Conclude by re-stating your position and summing up your arguments.
▶ Check your answer for errors and count the number of words you have used.

⊶ **ANSWERS PAGE 112**
PRACTICE TEST PAGE 105

The Speaking Test

An 11–14-minute test of your ability to speak English

How many parts does the speaking test have?
The speaking test has three parts as follows:

Part 1 (4–5 minutes)
You answer short questions from the examiner about yourself and everyday situations.

Part 2 (3–4 minutes)
You give a one- to two-minute talk, based on your own experience, on a simple topic provided by the examiner.

Part 3 (4–5 minutes)
You discuss some general but more abstract topics with the examiner that are related to the Part 2 talk.

Why are there different parts to the speaking test?
The test aims to find out whether you can express yourself in English on a variety of personal, general and abstract topics, using informal and formal language.

What is the speaking test like?
The test takes place at the authorised test centre where you enrolled, usually on the day of the written test.

There is only one examiner and one candidate in each IELTS speaking test.

The examiner will record the test. Don't worry about this. The recording is used for administrative purposes.

All examiners are trained and regularly checked to ensure that they conduct the test reliably. You should not know the examiner.

☐ ON THE DAY

- The speaking test usually takes place after the other parts of the test.

- Check your speaking test time and room with the administrator on the day.

- Take your passport (or photo identification as appropriate) with you so that you can show it to the examiner when he or she asks you. Take reading glasses, if you wear them. You do not need anything else.

- Arrive for the test early. You may be shown into a waiting room.

What general approach should I take to the speaking test?
Follow the examiner's instructions and listen carefully. Make sure you speak clearly and answer only the questions that you are asked. The examiner will know if you have memorised answers and you will lose marks for this.

How is the speaking test marked?

The speaking test is marked using a 9-band scale, like all other parts of the test. The examiner will be listening to four features of your language: fluency and coherence, vocabulary, grammar and accuracy, and pronunciation.

Fluency and coherence **Can you keep talking?** Can you speak clearly and smoothly without a lot of hesitation? Can you link your ideas using a range of words and expressions?	**Grammar and accuracy** **Is your speech accurate?** Can you use different types of structure? Can the examiner understand you even if you make mistakes?
Vocabulary **Do you know enough appropriate words?** Can you talk about yourself and about less familiar topics? Do you know how to vary your words and expressions to fit the topic?	**Pronunciation** **Do you pronounce words correctly?** Can the examiner understand everything you say? Do you use intonation and stress appropriately?

Is each part of the test marked separately?

No. The examiner conducts the test and marks you according to your performance across all three parts of the test.

What if I don't understand the examiner?

You can ask him or her to repeat the question or explain a word, e.g.

> *Sorry, could you repeat the question, please?*

OR

> *Could you explain what ... means?*

If you still don't understand, let the examiner go on to the next question. You may get more confused if you ask for another repetition.

What if I'm not sure about the answer?

Remember that the speaking test is a language test NOT a test of your views or general knowledge. You can use expressions that give you some time to think about how you will answer a question.

> *I'm not sure what I think about ...*
> *Let me think ...*
> *I really don't know / can't remember.*
> *It depends on ...*
> *I tend to think that ...*
> *On the whole, it seems that ...*

When do I get my result?

The examiner is not allowed to tell you anything about your performance. You will get your result when you receive your Test Report Form. This is usually two weeks after you have taken the test.

The Test Report Form will show your scores for all four parts of the test (Listening, Reading, Writing and Speaking) and your overall Band Score.

Speaking Part 1

Part 1	Four to five minutes	General questions about everyday situations
Part 2	Three to four minutes	Short talk about a simple topic
Part 3	Four to five minutes	Discussion of abstract topics

What is the purpose of Part 1?

The examiner wants to hear you answer questions on a few simple topics to find out if you can talk about yourself and everyday situations. Talking about personal topics is usually easier than talking about more abstract topics.

1 Look at these two questions. Tick the one you think is a Part 1 question.
  a What do you like about travelling by train?
  b To what extent has air travel replaced train travel?

How will the test begin?

The examiner will begin with some introductory questions. You should answer these questions briefly and clearly.

ON THE DAY

- Wait to be called into the exam room.

- When you go into the exam room, the examiner will tell you where to sit.

- The examiner will introduce you on the recording. He or she will say your name, candidate number and the centre name.

The examiner will ask you to say your name and ask you where you come from.
He or she will then ask to see your passport or photo identification.
The examiner does not need a long reply to the introductory questions.

What will happen next?

The examiner will introduce the first Part 1 topic, which is always about your home town or your studies/work.

2 Answer these questions about your home town.

> **a What**'s your home town called?
> **b Where** is it?
> **c How long** have you lived there?
> **d Do you like** living there? Why?
> **e Is there anything you dislike about** your home town?

3 Think of some other questions you could be asked about your studies/work using the words in bold above to help you.

What other topics will the examiner cover in Part 1?

You may get questions on any general, everyday topic, so you need to have some ideas. Normally the examiner will ask a few questions on three topics in total and will introduce each new topic clearly. So once you have answered a few questions on one topic, be prepared for a change of topic.

4 Complete the topic boxes below by thinking of three more ideas for each box.

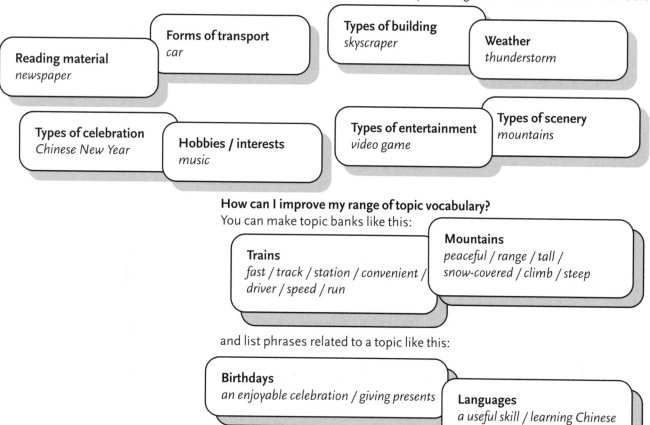

Reading material
newspaper

Forms of transport
car

Types of building
skyscraper

Weather
thunderstorm

Types of celebration
Chinese New Year

Hobbies / interests
music

Types of entertainment
video game

Types of scenery
mountains

How can I improve my range of topic vocabulary?

You can make topic banks like this:

Trains
fast / track / station / convenient / driver / speed / run

Mountains
peaceful / range / tall / snow-covered / climb / steep

and list phrases related to a topic like this:

Birthdays
an enjoyable celebration / giving presents

Languages
a useful skill / learning Chinese

5 Make some lists of words and phrases for the topic boxes in question 4 above.

6 Try to improve the way you describe things. Use one of these adjectives below in sentences a–i.

> impressive   depressing   enjoyable   complicated   relaxing
> informative   scary   sociable   tiring

a Some plane journeys are too long and ....
b The mountains near my home are high and very .... to look at.
c I learn from reading the newspaper because it's more .... than TV news.
d I find wet weather rather dull and ....
e Last year's Autumn Festival was a very .... occasion.
f The first time I went bungee jumping, it was pretty ....
g My uncle has lots of friends because he's a .... person.
h I prefer a .... holiday to an adventure holiday.
i I'm not very good at computer subjects because they seem so ....

7 Remember that words change their form depending on their use. Answer these questions using the correct form of the word in **bold**:

a Are you **prepared** for the test?
b How long does it take to **fly** to Mumbai?
c Is **pollution** a problem in Bangkok?
d Did the notes **help** you with the essay?
e Were you **free** to do as you liked at school?
f Do you dress for **comfort**?
g Do you play **golf**?
h Are there **crowds** of people on the trains?

a Yes, I've done lots of *preparation*.
b It's a seven-hour ....
c Yes, it's a very .... *city.*
d Yes, they were extremely ....
e No, we had very little ....
f Yes, I like wearing .... *clothes.*
g Yes, but I'm not a very good ....
h Yes, they're very ....

What sort of questions will the examiner ask?
The questions will be quite easy and will ask you to describe your likes and dislikes, your everyday life, your plans etc. You may have to talk about the past, present or future and you may have to give simple opinions.

8 Look at the questions below on the topic of holidays. Which question
   a asks about your likes/dislikes?
   b asks you about your personal preferences?
   c requires a past tense answer?
   d invites you to suggest reasons?
   e asks you how regularly you do something?
   f asks you to give a general view on the topic?
   g asks you to give an account?

A **How often** do you go on holiday?

B **How do you prefer** to travel when you go on holiday?

C **What do you enjoy doing** when you're on holiday?

D **Why do you think** people need to go on holiday?

E **Tell me about** your last holiday.

How long should my answers be?
In Part 1, your answers should not be very long, but try to give a full answer. You need to show that you can keep talking, without too much hesitation, and that you can link your ideas together. The examiner cannot give you high marks if your responses are always very short. Here is an example of a short answer and a good answer.

How often do you go on holiday?

Twice a year, usually.

*I usually go on holiday twice a year **but sometimes** I can only go once during the year **because** we are so busy at work. **So** it depends, really.*

9 Go back to question 8 and try to answer the questions there by giving a full response.

What if I can't think of anything to say?
Remember that Part 1 is about you. Draw on your own experience, and don't be afraid to say how you feel about something.

How can I improve my accuracy?
Listen carefully to the question, which will help you decide what tenses to use and how to form your answer. Here is an example of a past tense question and answer.

> How old were you when you left school?

> I **was** only 15 when I **left** my high school but I **went** back to college two years later.

10 Answer these questions using the correct tense and, where appropriate, try to give a full answer.

> **a** What's your favourite subject?
> **b** Where did you first learn English?
> **c** Do you prefer being taught in a small or a big class?
> **d** Are you planning to do any exams in the near future?
> **e** Have you ever been in a school play?
> **f** Has your government made any recent changes in schools?

11 Find the errors in these answers and correct them.

> **a** Where do you come from?
> **b** How do you spend your leisure time?
> **c** Are you interested in fashion?
> **d** Do you live with your family or with friends?
> **e** What do you find difficult about learning English?
> **f** What do you enjoy about your course?
> **g** What are your plans for next year?
> **h** When do people in your country take holidays?
> **i** Do you like fruit?

> **a** I came from Tokyo.
> **b** I will play basketball.
> **c** Yes. I'm like fashion very much.
> **d** I'm living with my family since I'm born.
> **e** I am not easy to pronounce English words.
> **f** I enjoy discussing about economics.
> **g** I'm thinking to go to America.
> **h** Most of people go away in the summer.
> **i** I don't eat many fruit.

ACTION PLAN

▶ Respond briefly to the introductory questions.
▶ Make sure you can talk about your home town and your studies or work.
▶ Build some lists of phrases and topic banks.
▶ Listen to the question forms and the words that the examiner uses. These will help you form your answer.
▶ Try to give a full answer. The examiner wants to listen to you speak, so remember: it is important to talk.
▶ Don't memorise long answers. You will lose marks for this.
▶ Answer each question directly. Don't talk about something unrelated to the examiner's question.

⊶ ANSWERS PAGE 113
PRACTICE TEST PAGE 106

Speaking Part 2

Part 1	Four to five minutes	General questions about everyday situations
Part 2	**Three to four minutes**	**Short talk about a simple topic**
Part 3	Four to five minutes	Discussion of abstract topics

What is the purpose of Part 2?
The examiner wants to hear you give a short talk about a simple topic based on your own experience, to see whether you can speak for one to two minutes on your own.

When does Part 2 begin?
When you have answered the last question in Part 1, the examiner will introduce Part 2.

The examiner will introduce Part 2 by saying: *Now, I'm going to give you a topic and I'd like you to talk about it for one to two minutes.*

Then the examiner will give you a piece of paper and a pen or pencil to make notes, and your topic. You will have one minute to prepare your talk.

Do I need to time myself in the test?
No. The examiner will time all the parts of the test. When you do the Part 2 talk, he or she will stop you when you have talked for a maximum of two minutes. However, you do need to have an idea of how long two minutes is, so that you can plan your talk.

What does the Part 2 topic look like?
The text will clearly state the topic that you need to talk about and will give some points to guide your talk.

The box on the left is an example of a topic.

> Describe a scientific development that has benefited mankind.
>
> You should say:
>   what type of development it is
>   why it was needed
>   how it has been used
>
> and explain why this scientific development was so beneficial.

1 Underline the topic, and the points that you need to cover in your talk.

What if I don't understand some of the words in the topic?
You can ask the examiner to explain any words you don't understand.

How long will I have to make notes?
The examiner will give you one minute to make some notes. During this time, he or she will not talk to you. The notes are not marked and will be thrown away after the test. You cannot take them out of the room.

What if I haven't got any experience of the topic?

Use your imagination and invent some ideas. Remember that the examiner is testing your ability to speak English, not your views or general knowledge.

2 Here are six possible topics. Take two minutes to read through topics A–F and write down two ideas from your own experience for each one.
   A An activity that you enjoy.
   B An exciting experience from your childhood.
   C A person that you would like to meet.
   D A celebration that took place in your home town.
   E A job that you have done.
   F A play or concert that you have been in.

How can I make sure I choose a good idea to talk about?

The three points often begin with *How* or *Wh-* question words such as *why, who, when, whether, what* or *which*. These points are given to help you.

3 Read the topic in the box on the left and the start of the student's talk. What mistake has he made?

> Describe a plan you have made for your future that is not related to your studies.
>
> You should say:
>   what the plan is
>   when you think you will do it
>   how it could change your life
>
> and explain why you have made this plan.

I think I'll talk about getting married – that'll be easy.

I'm going to talk about my plan to get married. Er, I want to get married before I'm 30... Er, it'll change my life, obviously, er, because I won't be single any more... Er, I can't think...

4 Think of two plans you could talk about. Take about one minute to make an idea map, like the one below, for each plan.

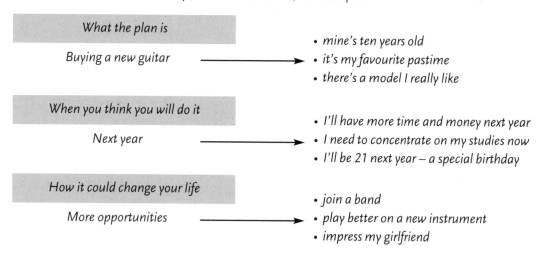

What the plan is	
Buying a new guitar	→ • mine's ten years old • it's my favourite pastime • there's a model I really like

When you think you will do it	
Next year	→ • I'll have more time and money next year • I need to concentrate on my studies now • I'll be 21 next year – a special birthday

How it could change your life	
More opportunities	→ • join a band • play better on a new instrument • impress my girlfriend

5 Which of your plans do you think will be easier to talk about? Why?

Should I talk about the points in order?

You can cover the points in any order. You may have more to say about some points than others. This doesn't matter.

What tense should I speak in?

This will depend on the instructions. The tense may change through your talk depending on the points you are given.

6 Underline or highlight all the different verb tenses in the talk below on 'an activity that you enjoy'.

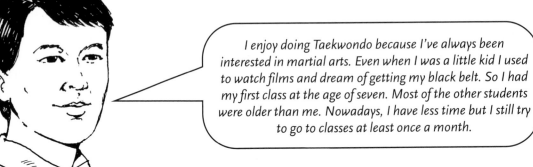

> I enjoy doing Taekwondo because I've always been interested in martial arts. Even when I was a little kid I used to watch films and dream of getting my black belt. So I had my first class at the age of seven. Most of the other students were older than me. Nowadays, I have less time but I still try to go to classes at least once a month.

7 What points do you think the student was given to talk about?

How should I start my talk?

When the minute's preparation time is over, the examiner will tell you to begin. Your opening words should tell the examiner what you have chosen to talk about.

8 Fill in the gaps in the talks below using an appropriate verb in an appropriate tense. You can use more than one word for each space and choose your own verbs. Then read the talks aloud.

> **A** I'm going to talk about my first job.
> I .... in a small village in the countryside, but soon after that, my family moved to Bangkok and I .... there until I .... my studies. I got used to the big city so after that I .... abroad to work for a multinational company. This job ....

> **B** The person I'd like to meet is the president of our country because he .... a very important person. He's .... by the people and .... in office for five years. I think it .... an honour to meet him and I .... very proud.

> **C** I'd like to talk about the royal wedding that took place in Copenhagen in 2004. The Prince of Denmark .... married to a young woman from Australia, and I .... lucky enough to be in Copenhagen at the time of the wedding. Thousands of people .... out onto the streets to watch the couple go past in an open carriage. Even though I .... believe in fairy tales, this .... a real fairy-tale wedding.

How can I show a range of topic vocabulary?
Make a mind map of some of the vocabulary and ideas you can use. The examiner will be listening to see whether you know a range of words related to the topic. Use as many as you can and don't worry too much about making mistakes. Imagine this is your topic.

Describe an adventure from your childhood.

You should say:
where you were
who you were with
what happened

and explain why you think it was an adventure.

I think I'll talk about when I was rescued by a helicopter… hiking with friends… broke my ankle… yes… good idea!

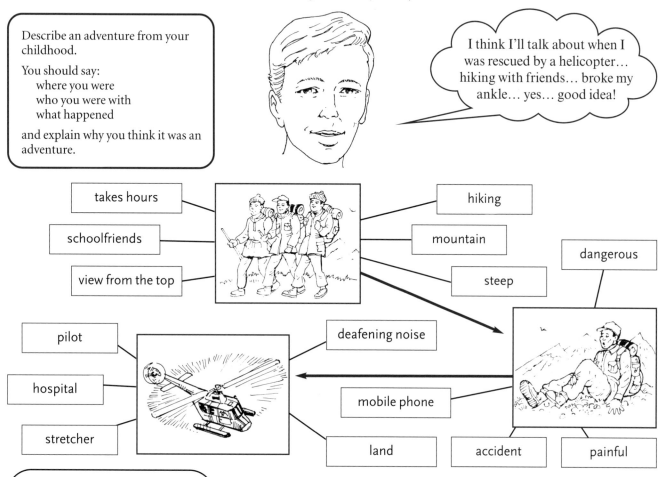

takes hours

schoolfriends

view from the top

hiking

mountain

steep

dangerous

pilot

hospital

stretcher

deafening noise

mobile phone

land

accident

painful

I'm going to talk about when I went **(a)** …….. with some of my **(b)** …….. in the French Alps. Er, it was a school holiday and so we decided to climb a famous **(c)** …….. called La Tournette. It's not difficult but it **(d)** …….. to get up to the top and there are a couple of places where it's rather **(e)** …….. . But it's worth it because the **(f)** …….. is incredible. Even in warm weather, you can find snow there, too.

9 Use some of the words in the mind map to complete the first part of the student's talk on the left.

ACTION PLAN

▶ Read the whole topic carefully first.
▶ Choose an idea that you can talk about for up to two minutes.
▶ Think about the tenses you will use.
▶ Prepare some ideas for the whole talk, not just the opening.
▶ Don't talk about something unrelated to the topic.
▶ Introduce your topic clearly at the start of your talk.

ANSWERS PAGE 114
PRACTICE TEST PAGE 106

Speaking Part 3

Part 1	Four to five minutes	General questions about everyday situations
Part 2	Three to four minutes	Short talk about a simple topic
Part 3	**Four to five minutes**	**Discussion of abstract topics**

What is the purpose of Part 3?
The examiner wants to hear you discuss some general but more abstract topics that are related to the Part 2 talk.

When does Part 3 begin?
At the end of your two-minute talk, the examiner will lead you into Part 3 by asking you about a more general aspect of the topic.

The examiner may ask a quick question on your Part 2 talk, e.g. *Have you always wanted to visit this place?* You need only give a short *Yes* or *No* answer. He or she will then introduce the Part 3 discussion by referring back to your Part 2 talk, e.g. *We've been talking about a place you'd like to visit and I'd like to discuss with you one or two more general questions related to this.*

What is an abstract topic?
How much time you spend watching television is about you and is a Part 1 topic. *Whether television has a negative effect on people* is more general and abstract and is a Part 3 topic.

1 Which of the following topics are Part 3 topics?
   a the impact of technology on work
   b your favourite newspaper
   c the effects of modern farming methods
   d teenage attitudes to parents
   e how you keep fit
   f whether competition is a positive thing
   g how your family celebrates Chinese New Year
   h why some children's stories are popular

What sort of questions will the examiner ask?
The examiner will ask a range of questions based on the topic from Part 2. The first question often asks you to describe or outline your views on a general aspect of this topic.

The examiner may begin with a question like this.

> In your view, what are some of the benefits of travelling to new places?

> *The personal topic of 'a place I'd like to visit' has become a more general topic about travel. This is the sort of change I should expect in Part 3.*

2 What are the key words in the question?

3 What could the student do to improve this response?

> *For a start, it can be very exciting, and it can also be personally rewarding.*

If you give a short reply, the examiner will ask more questions to help you develop your answer. He or she may stress some words to help you.

> What would you find **particularly** exciting about going to a new country?

> **In what way** is it personally rewarding?

What strategy can I use to produce a good answer?
You need to focus on the key words in the question, and produce two or three ideas which you can support.

4 Look at this exchange between an examiner and a student, who has not provided enough language for the examiner to make a judgement about their level.

> Do older people learn as much from travelling as younger people?

> *Yes, of course they do. I think it's the same.*

Here are some useful strategies for developing ideas. Use the words provided to help you build a better answer to the question above.

Think about what other people might believe.	*Even though some people .... I think ....*
Make a direct contrast or comparison.	*I tend to think that while young people, ... older people ....*
Use personal experience.	*It's hard to say, but in my experience .... and so I think ....*
Refer back in time.	*I think in the past it was true that .... but nowadays ....*
Refer to the media.	*Newspapers and other media suggest that young people don't .... but I'm not sure they're right ....*
Analyse the question.	*I think it depends on the type of person. If the young person is .... , then .... but if they are .... , then ....*
Agree or disagree.	*Generally I would say that they do, but there are young people who ....*

5 Here is a response to the question *Who else benefits from the fact that people like to travel?* Which key idea does the student develop?

> I think there can be lots of benefits for everyone... benefits for the person travelling and also for the people who live there, because many countries rely on tourism and so it's good when lots of visitors come. It provides work for the local people.

How does Part 3 progress?

The questions will become more difficult. You can improve your answers in Part 3 if you understand how the topic is being developed and what abstract ideas might be related to it. Here is an example of a model chain of questions, which an examiner might ask about a topic.

Part 2 topic	Part 3 ideas
An activity that you enjoy.	Leisure centres / the role of sport in society / global sporting events

> How important is it for people to have a hobby?

> Do you think that there is too much emphasis on sport in our society today?

> Do global sporting events, such as the Olympic Games, have a role in the 21st century?

6 Try to think of possible Part 3 ideas for these two topics.

Part 2 topic	Part 3 ideas
A job that you have done.	
A play or concert that you have been in.	

7 Write down a few questions that the examiner could ask you on these two topics. Try to make them progressively more difficult.

How long should my answers be?

The examiner can only assess what you say, so it's important to give a full and relevant answer, linking your ideas smoothly. This skill is known as fluency.

How can I improve my fluency?

When you give an opinion, try to back it up by giving a reason for it or by offering a second point of view. Here are some useful expressions for doing this.

For me .... is very important	because ....
I think	but I can understand that ....
I don't really think much of	On the other hand ....
It all depends	Personally I believe ....
Some people feel	But I actually think ....

8 Complete the following answers to the examiner's three questions on page 90.

> *For me, having a hobby is ....
> because ....*

> *Some people feel that sport is a waste of
> time because ....
> But I actually think ....*

> *I don't really think the Olympic Games
> are .... On the other hand, the FIFA World
> Cup is always fantastic. I really ....*

How can I improve my pronunciation score?

You should speak loudly enough for the examiner to hear you, and try to pronounce your words clearly. Pay attention to the way you emphasise words and syllables within words, and try not to speak in a monotonous voice.

How can I identify my pronunciation weaknesses?

You can record your answers to any of the speaking exercises in this book and ask a teacher or a native speaker of English to help you identify your problem areas.

ACTION PLAN

▶ Give a full answer to each question and take the initiative.
▶ Think about how topics can be developed so that you are ready to explore the questions you are asked.
▶ Answer each question directly. Don't talk about something unrelated to the examiner's question.
▶ Try to link your ideas, so that your speech flows well.

⊶ **ANSWERS PAGE 114**
PRACTICE TEST PAGE 107

Practice Test

LISTENING

SECTION 1   Questions 1–10

Questions 1–3
Choose **THREE** letters **B–H**.

Which **THREE** other activities does the customer want to do?

Example   Ⓐ visit family
            B save money
            C study geography
            D study English
            E do some winter sports
            F go sailing
            G join a walking tour
            H meet young people

Questions 4–7
Complete the form below.

Write **NO MORE THAN THREE WORDS AND/OR A NUMBER** for each answer.

——— CUSTOMER'S DETAILS ———	
Name	*Su Ming Lee* ....
Address	**4** .... *Kew*
Mobile	**5** *0402* ....
Day and date of departure	**6** ....
Length of course	**7** ....
Method of payment	*credit card* ....

Questions 8–10
Label the map opposite.

Write the correct letter **A–G** next to questions 8–10.

8 The language school is at ……

9 The hotel is at ……

10 The bookshop is at ……

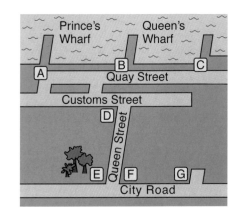

🔑 **ANSWERS PAGE 115**
      RECORDING SCRIPTS PAGE 118

SECTION 2   Questions 11–20

Questions 11–13
Complete the sentences below.

*Write **NO MORE THAN THREE WORDS** for each answer.*

11 .... are often known by their famous bridges.

12 The speaker compares a bridge to a cathedral or ....

13 Sydney Harbour Bridge is nicknamed ....

Questions 14–18
Complete the table below.

*Write **NO MORE THAN THREE WORDS AND/OR A NUMBER** for each answer.*

Date	Event
1916	**14** .... agreed to finance bridge
15	Contract signed with engineering firm
1926	Construction involved: • knocking down **16** .... • creation of many jobs
1932	Bridge completed at a cost of **17** £ ....
March 1932	Opening ceremony Ribbon cut by a man riding a **18** ....

Questions 19–20
Answer the questions below.

*Write **NO MORE THAN THREE WORDS AND/OR A NUMBER** for each answer.*

19 How long is the tunnel?

....

20 Name **ONE** thing the tunnel can withstand.

....

⊶ **ANSWERS PAGE 115**
RECORDING SCRIPTS PAGE 119

SECTION 3 Questions 21–30

Question 21
*Choose the correct letter **A**, **B** or **C**.*

21 Which graph shows the distribution of animals painted on the caves?

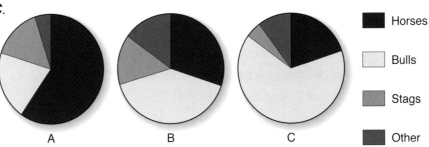

Questions 22–25
How does the woman describe each type of drawing?

*Choose your answers from the box and write the letters **A–H** next to questions 22–25.*

22 bulls ....

23 humans ....

24 signs ....

25 fish ....

A uncommon	**E** consisting of dots
B realistic	**F** complex
C two-dimensional	**G** important
D childish	**H** huge

Questions 26–27
Label the diagram below.

*Write **NO MORE THAN THREE WORDS** for each answer.*

27 ....

26 ....

Chamber of Felines

Chamber of Engravings

Lateral Passage

Great Hall of the Bulls

Questions 28–30
*Choose the correct letter **A**, **B** or **C**.*

28 The cave was closed in 1963 because
  A the tourists had drawn pictures on the walls.
  B the air was harming the rock art.
  C so few people were visiting the site.

29 How does David feel about the closure of the cave?
  A He agrees with the decision.
  B He thinks it was a bad idea.
  C He has no views on the matter.

30 How can people enjoy the drawings today?
  A The government has re-opened the cave.
  B The drawings have been photographed.
  C A replica of the cave has been built.

ANSWERS PAGE 115
RECORDING SCRIPTS PAGE 120

SECTION 4   Questions 31–40

Questions 31–32
Complete the notes below.

Write **NO MORE THAN THREE WORDS** *for each answer.*

What is marketing?

31 .... and .... represent only two aspects of marketing.

Marketing involves

• finding customers

• ensuring customer satisfaction

• **32** ....

Questions 33–34
Complete the flow chart below.

Write **NO MORE THAN TWO WORDS** *for each answer.*

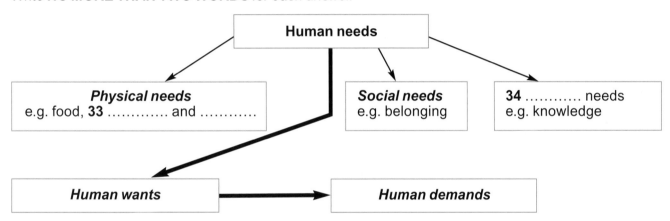

Questions 35–38
Which market research method is used by each of these businesses?

Write the correct letter **A–C** *next to questions 35–38.*

A customer observation	**35** supermarkets ....
B free offers	**36** department stores ....
C in-store surveys	**37** fast-food companies ....
	38 theme parks ....

Questions 39–40
Complete the notes below.

Write **NO MORE THAN THREE WORDS** *for each answer.*

Customer satisfaction

Product performance	Customers are
• poor • good • **40**	• unhappy • **39** .... • delighted

ANSWERS PAGE 115
RECORDING SCRIPTS PAGE 121

ACADEMIC READING

READING PASSAGE 1

*You should spend about 20 minutes on **questions 1–13**, which are based on Reading Passage 1 below.*

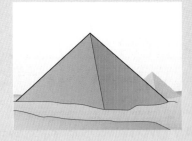

The people of ancient Egypt emerged as one of the first Western civilisations. Sustained by the River Nile and protected by vast deserts, the Egyptians lived in comparative security, prosperity and peace for thousands of years. When such conditions exist, the civilisation and its arts usually flourish. To this day, many of the Egyptian artistic creations display the wealth, splendour and talent of this great civilisation.

Ancient Egypt has been called a land of temples and tombs, and for centuries people have been filled with wonder at the ingenuity of the Egyptians, whose impressive works have withstood the ravages of time so well. Had it not been for the long-lasting nature of their monuments and carved inscriptions in the form of hieroglyphics[1], much evidence of their activities would have vanished from all historical records. In about 3000 BC, Upper and Lower Egypt were united under the first pharaoh[2], and generally from that time until the invasion by Alexander the Great in 332 BC, Egypt prospered as a nation of skilful craftsmen and artists.

The Egyptians were an industrious, highly civilised and deeply religious people, who obediently accepted the supreme authority of their pharaohs. The people were content to serve and work for the state in return for a secure livelihood. They considered this earthly life to be a segment in a great cycle, at the end of which everything would be returned to its original form. The richer and more important the person, the more careful and elaborate would be his or her burial, and the stronger and safer the tomb in which they would be buried.

The burial of the dead in the ground was not considered sufficiently safe for kings, queens and court officials, so sunken, sealed tombs were ingeniously constructed to protect personal treasures, food and instructions for the safe conduct of the soul after death. The design of these tombs developed into the stepped pyramid, and finally into the square pyramid that we know today.

There are about 80 ancient pyramids in Egypt. The Great Pyramid at Gizeh, which King Cheops built as his tomb 5000 years ago, holds most interest. It stands with two other pyramids on a slight rise overlooking the River Nile. At the centre of the pyramid is the King's Chamber and leading down from there is a long narrow area known as the Grand Gallery. The pyramid covers 13 acres and contains 2,300,000 blocks of limestone, each weighing an average of 1.5 tons. Its pyramidal form has a perfectly square base with sides of 756 feet and a height of 481 feet. Situated directly below the King's Chamber is the Queen's

[1] hieroglyphics = pictorial writing system used by the ancient Egyptians

[2] pharaoh = king

Chamber and there are two air channels leading upwards from the centre of the pyramid to the outside.

Originally the exterior was covered in highly polished limestone slabs, all of which have been stolen over the years. It is estimated that a total of 100,000 men laboured for 20 years to build this gigantic structure, and although architecturally unimportant in design, it has aroused the curiosity of millions of people because of the uncanny accuracy of its measurements and proportions. It reveals the remarkable ingenuity and the great organising ability of the ancient Egyptians.

Near these pyramids stands the Great Sphinx, the origin and purpose of which constitute one of the world's most famous puzzles. Shaped from an outcrop of stone in the form of a human-headed lion, the face is possibly a portrait of King Khafra, the son of Cheops, who was buried in the second largest pyramid. The Sphinx is one of the biggest statues ever made.

The Egyptian people showed reverence towards natural objects such as the lotus flower, the scarab beetle, the falcon, the lion, the sun and the River Nile. All these subjects and many more were used symbolically and conventionally as motifs in low-relief carving and painting. It was the custom of the Egyptians to depict the various parts of the human figure, usually in the most characteristic positions. The head was shown in profile except for the eye, which was represented from the front, the shoulders and a portion of the arms were portrayed from the front, while the hips and legs were side views. Wall decoration showed little or no attempt to indicate depth or perspective, except by placing distant objects above near things. It was essentially two-dimensional, and relative size indicated the status of the person, so the pharaoh was the largest figure in the composition.

Egyptian art is characterised by a passion for permanence, a desire to impress by size, and a determination to make each item serve its function without much regard for the whole. It is obvious that art among these people reached a very high level and the strong influence of Egyptian art can be seen in the work of nearby civilisations.

The fortunate discovery and subsequent deciphering in 1822 of the Rosetta Stone, which showed the same laws inscribed both in Egyptian hieroglyphics and the Egyptian demotic, or popular version of their language, as well as the Greek language, eventually gave the key to the meaning of Egyptian inscriptions, and therefore the significance of much Egyptian art.

Questions 1–3
Complete the sentences below.

*Choose **NO MORE THAN THREE WORDS** from the passage for each answer.*

Write your answers in boxes 1–3 on your answer sheet.

1 Security and peace are two .... that are necessary for a civilisation to be successful.

2 Ancient Egyptians worked as both ....

3 Ordinary Egyptians expected to receive .... for their hard work.

Questions 4–7

Label the diagram below.

*Choose **NO MORE THAN THREE WORDS AND/OR NUMBERS** from the passage for each answer.*

Write your answers in boxes 4–7 on your answer sheet.

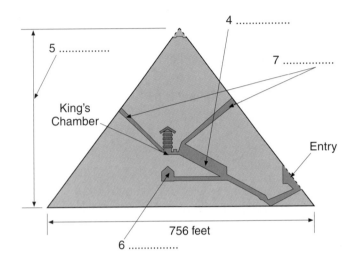

Questions 8–12

Do the following statements agree with the information given in Reading Passage 1?

In boxes 8–12 on your answer sheet write

TRUE   *if the statement agrees with the information*
FALSE   *if the statement contradicts the information*
NOT GIVEN *if there is no information on this*

8   The surface of the Great Pyramid is covered in polished limestone slabs.

9   King Khafra died before King Cheops.

10 Egyptian carvings were often based on things found in nature.

11 Important characters in Egyptian carvings were bigger than less important characters.

12 Egyptian art was greatly influenced by the art of neighbouring cultures.

Question 13

*Choose the correct letter **A**, **B**, **C** or **D**.*

Write the correct letter in box 13 on your answer sheet.

The writer's aim in this passage is to

A describe the construction methods of the pyramids.
B explain the beliefs of the ancient Egyptians.
C offer an interpretation of Egyptian art and sculpture.
D provide an overview of early Egyptian society.

READING PASSAGE 2

*You should spend about 20 minutes on **questions 14–26**, which are based on Reading Passage 2 below.*

Sticking power

Want to walk on the ceiling?
All it takes is a bit of fancy footwork

A If Kellar Autumn, an expert in biomechanics at Clark College in Portland, Oregon, has his way, the first footprints on Mars won't be human. They'll belong to a gecko. Gecko toes have legendary sticking power – and the Clark College scientist would like to see the next generation of Martian robots walking about on gecko-style feet. A gecko can whiz up the smoothest wall and hang from the ceiling by one foot, with no fear of falling.

B Autumn is one of a long line of researchers who have puzzled over the gecko's gravity-defying footwork. Earlier this year, he and his colleagues discovered that the gecko's toes don't just stick, they bond to the surface beneath them. Engineers are already trying to copy the gecko's technique – but reptilian feet are not the only ones they are interested in.

C Some of the most persistent 'hanging' creatures are insects. They can defy not just gravity, but gusts of wind, raindrops and a predator's attempt to prize them loose. Recent discoveries about how they achieve this could lead to the development of quick-release adhesives and miniature grippers, ideal for manipulating microscopic components or holding tiny bits of tissue together during surgery. 'There are lots of ways to make two surfaces stick together, but there are very few which provide precise and reversible attachment,' says Stas Gorb, a biologist in Tübingen, Germany, working on the problem.

D Geckos and insects have both perfected ways of doing this, and engineers and scientists would dearly love to know how. Friction certainly plays a part in assisting horizontal movement, but when the animal is running up a slope, climbing vertically or travelling upside down, it needs a more powerful adhesive. Just what that adhesive is has been hotly debated for years. Some people suggested that insects had micro-suckers. Some reckoned they relied on electrostatic forces. Others thought that intermolecular forces between pad and leaf might provide a firm foothold.

E Most of the evidence suggests that insects rely on 'wet adhesion', hanging on with the help of a thin film of fluid on the bottom of the pad. Insects often leave tiny trails of oily footprints. Some clearly secrete a fluid onto the 'soles' of their feet. And they tend to lose their footing when they have their feet cleaned or dried.

F This year, Walter Federle, an entomologist at the University of Würzburg, showed experimentally that an insect's sticking power depends on a thin film of liquid under its feet. He placed an ant on a polished turntable inside the rotor of a centrifuge, and switched it on. At slow speeds, the ant carried on walking unperturbed. But as the scientist slowly increased the speed, the pulling forces grew stronger and the ant stopped dead, legs spread out and all six feet planted firmly on the ground. At higher speeds still, the ant's feet began to slide. 'This can only be explained by the presence of a liquid,' says Federle. 'If the ant relied on some form of dry adhesion, its feet would pop abruptly off the surface once the pull got too strong.'

G But the liquid isn't the whole story. What engineers really find exciting about insect feet is the way they make almost perfect contact with the surface beneath. 'Sticking to a perfectly smooth surface is no big deal,' says Gorb. But in nature, even the smoothest-looking surfaces have microscopic lumps and bumps. For a footpad to make good contact, it must follow the contours of the landscape beneath it. Flies, beetles and earwigs have solved the problem with hairy footpads, with hairs that bend like the bristles of a toothbrush to accommodate the troughs below.

H Gorb has tested dozens of species with this sort of pad to see which had the best stick. Flies resist a pull of three or four times their body weight – perfectly adequate for crossing the ceiling. But beetles can do better and the champion is a small, blue beetle with oversized yellow feet, found in the south-eastern parts of the US.

I Tom Eisner, a chemical ecologist at Cornell University in New York, has been fascinated by this beetle for years. Almost 30 years ago, he suggested that the beetle clung on tight to avoid being picked off by predators – ants in particular. When Eisner measured the beetle's sticking power earlier this year, he found that it can withstand pulling forces of around 80 times its own weight for about two minutes and an astonishing 200 times its own weight for shorter periods. 'The ants give up because the beetle holds on longer than they can be bothered to attack it,' he says.

J Whatever liquid insects rely on, the gecko seems able to manage without it. No one knows quite why the gecko needs so much sticking power. 'It seems overbuilt for the job,' says Autumn. But whatever the gecko's needs are, its skills are in demand by humans. Autumn and his colleagues in Oregon have already helped to create a robot that walks like a gecko. Mecho-Gecko, a robot built by iRobot of Massachusetts, walks like a lizard – rolling its toes down and peeling them up again. At the moment, though, it has to make do with balls of glue to give it stick. The next step is to try to reproduce the hairs on a gecko's toes and create a robot with the full set of gecko skills. Then we could build robots with feet that stick without glue, clean themselves and work just as well underwater as in the vacuum of space, or crawling over the dusty landscape of Mars.

Questions 14–18

Look at the following statements (Questions 14–18) and the list of scientists below.

*Match each statement with the correct scientist **A**, **B**, **C** or **D**.*

*Write the correct letter **A**, **B**, **C** or **D** in boxes 14–18 on your answer sheet.*

14 Some insects use their ability to stick to surfaces as a way of defending themselves.

15 What makes sticky insect feet special is the fact that they can also detach themselves easily from a surface.

16 Gecko feet seem to be stickier than they need to be.

17 A robot with gecko-style feet would be ideal for exploring other planets.

18 Evidence shows that in order to stick, insect feet have to be wet.

List of Scientists
A Kellar Autumn
B Stas Gorb
C Walter Federle
D Tom Eisner

Questions 19–22

Reading Passage 2 has ten paragraphs **A–J**.

Which paragraph contains the following information?

*Write the correct letter **A–J** in boxes 19–22 on your answer sheet.*

19 some of the practical things a gecko-style adhesive could be used for

20 a description of a test involving an insect in motion

21 three different theories scientists have had about how insect feet stick

22 examples of remarkable gecko movements

Questions 23–26

*Complete each sentence with the correct ending **A–G** below.*

*Write the correct letter **A–G** in boxes 23–26 on your answer sheet.*

23 Insect feet lose their sticking power when they

24 If you put ants on a rapidly rotating object, their feet

25 Beetles can stick to uneven surfaces because they

26 The toes on robots like Mecho-Gecko

A stick to surfaces in and out of water.

B curl up and down.

C are washed and dried.

D resist a pull of three times their body weight.

E start to slip across the surface.

F leave yellow footprints.

G have hairy footpads.

READING PASSAGE 3

*You should spend about 20 minutes on **questions 27–40**, which are based on Reading Passage 3 on the next page.*

Questions 27–32

Reading Passage 3 has seven paragraphs **A–G**.

*Choose the correct heading for paragraphs **B–G** from the list of headings below.*

*Write the correct number **i–x** in boxes 27–32 on your answer sheet.*

List of Headings

i Why some early social science methods lost popularity

ii The cost implications of research

iii Looking ahead to an unbiased assessment of research

iv A range of social issues that have been usefully studied

v An example of a poor decision that was made too quickly

vi What happens when the figures are wrong

vii One area of research that is rigorously carried out

viii The changing nature of medical trials

ix An investigative study that may lead to a new system

x Why some scientists' theories are considered second-rate

Example Paragraph **A**	Answer **x**

27 Paragraph **B**   **30** Paragraph **E**

28 Paragraph **C**   **31** Paragraph **F**

29 Paragraph **D**   **32** Paragraph **G**

TRY IT AND SEE

In the social sciences, it is often supposed that there can be no such thing as a controlled experiment. Think again.

A In the scientific pecking order, social scientists are usually looked down on by their peers in the natural sciences. Natural scientists do experiments to test their theories or, if they cannot, they try to look for natural phenomena that can act in lieu of experiments. Social scientists, it is widely thought, do not subject their own hypotheses to any such rigorous treatment. Worse, they peddle their untested hypotheses to governments and try to get them turned into policies.

B Governments require sellers of new medicines to demonstrate their safety and effectiveness. The accepted gold standard of evidence is a randomised control trial, in which a new drug is compared with the best existing therapy (or with a placebo, if no treatment is available). Patients are assigned to one arm or the other of such a study at random, ensuring that the only difference between the two groups is the new treatment. The best studies also ensure that neither patient nor physician knows which patient is allocated to which therapy. Drug trials must also include enough patients to make it unlikely that chance alone may determine the result.

C But few education programmes or social initiatives are evaluated in carefully conducted studies prior to their introduction. A case in point is the 'whole-language' approach to reading, which swept much of the English-speaking world in the 1970s and 1980s. The whole-language theory holds that children learn to read best by absorbing contextual clues from texts, not by breaking individual words into their component parts and reassembling them (a method known as phonics). Unfortunately, the educational theorists who pushed the whole-language notion so successfully did not wait for evidence from controlled randomised trials before advancing their claims. Had they done so, they might have concluded, as did an analysis of 52 randomised studies carried out by the US National Reading Panel in 2000, that effective reading instruction requires phonics.

D To avoid the widespread adoption of misguided ideas, the sensible thing is to experiment first and make policy later. This is the idea behind a trial of restorative justice which is taking place in the English courts. The experiment will include criminals who plead guilty to robbery. Those who agree to participate will be assigned randomly either to sentencing as normal or to participation in a conference in which the offender comes face-to-face with his victim and discusses how he may make emotional and material restitution. The purpose of the trial is to assess whether such restorative justice limits re-offending. If it does, it might be adopted more widely.

E The idea of experimental evidence is not quite as new to the social sciences as sneering natural scientists might believe. In fact, randomised trials and systematic reviews of evidence were introduced into the social sciences long before they became common in medicine. An apparent example of random allocation is a study carried out in 1927 of how to persuade people to vote in elections. And randomised trials in social work were begun in the 1930s and 1940s. But enthusiasm later waned. This loss of interest can be attributed, at least in part, to the fact that early experiments produced little evidence of positive outcomes. Others suggest that much of the opposition to experimental evaluation stems from a common philosophical malaise among social scientists, who doubt the validity of the natural sciences, and therefore reject the potential of knowledge derived from controlled experiments. A more pragmatic factor limiting the growth of evidence-based education and social services may be limitations on the funds available for research.

F Nevertheless, some 11,000 experimental studies are known in the social sciences (compared with over 250,000 in the medical literature). Randomised trials have been used to evaluate the effectiveness of driver-education programmes, job-training schemes, classroom size, psychological counselling for post-traumatic stress disorder and increased investment in public housing. And where they are carried out, they seem to have a healthy dampening effect on otherwise rosy interpretations of the observations.

G The problem for policymakers is often not too few data, but what to make of multiple and conflicting studies. This is where a body called the Campbell Collaboration comes into its own. This independent non-profit organisation is designed to evaluate existing studies, in a process known as a systematic review. This means attempting to identify every relevant trial of a given question (including studies that have never been published), choosing the best ones using clearly defined criteria for quality, and combining the results in a statistically valid way. An equivalent body, the Cochrane Collaboration, has produced more than 1,000 such reviews in medical fields. The hope is that rigorous review standards will allow Campbell, like Cochrane, to become a trusted and authoritative source of information.

Questions 33–36

Complete the summary below.

*Choose **NO MORE THAN TWO WORDS** from the passage for each answer.*

Write your answers in boxes 33–36 on your answer sheet.

Fighting Crime

Some criminals in England are agreeing to take part in a trial designed to help reduce their chances of **33** .... The idea is that while one group of randomly selected criminals undergoes the usual **34** .... , the other group will discuss the possibility of making some repayment for the crime by meeting the **35** .... It is yet to be seen whether this system, known as **36** .... , will work.

Questions 37–40

Classify the following characteristics as relating to

   A *Social Science*
   B *Medical Science*
   C *Both Social Science and Medical Science*
   D *Neither Social Science nor Medical Science*

*Write the correct letter **A**, **B**, **C** or **D** in boxes 37–40 on your answer sheet.*

37 a tendency for negative results in early trials

38 the desire to submit results for independent assessment

39 the prioritisation of research areas to meet government needs

40 the widespread use of studies that investigate the quality of new products

🔑 **ANSWERS PAGE 115**

ACADEMIC WRITING

WRITING TASK 1

You should spend about 20 minutes on this task.

> **The diagram below shows how a central heating system in a house works.**
>
> **Summarise the information by selecting and reporting the main features, and make comparisons where relevant.**

Write at least 150 words.

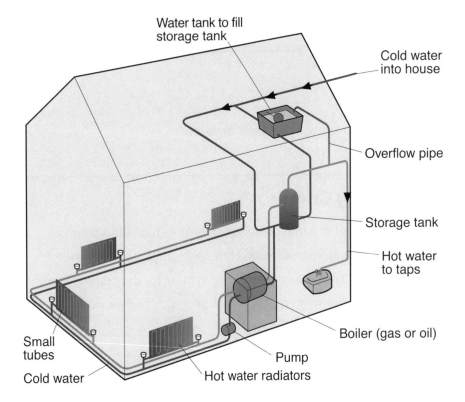

Water tank to fill storage tank

Cold water into house

Overflow pipe

Storage tank

Hot water to taps

Boiler (gas or oil)

Small tubes

Pump

Cold water

Hot water radiators

⚷ Read the sample answer on page 115 and go through the checklist.

	✔	Comments
Is there an introduction to the diagram?		
Is there an overview?		
Can you underline the key features?		
Can you underline the supporting information?		
Are the paragraph breaks in the right place?		
Can you identify the linkers and reference words?		
Can you identify the topic vocabulary?		
Is the answer the right length?		

WRITING TASK 2

You should spend about 40 minutes on this task.

Write about the following topic:

> *The number of overweight children in developed countries is increasing. Some people think this is due to problems such as the growing number of fast food outlets. Others believe that parents are to blame for not looking after their children's health.*
>
> *To what extent do you agree with these views?*

Give reasons for your answer and include any relevant examples from your own knowledge or experience.

Write at least 250 words.

⚷ Read the sample answer on page 116 and go through the checklist.

	✔	Comments
Can you identify the writer's position?		
Can you underline the main ideas in each paragraph?		
Can you identify the linkers and reference words?		
Can you identify the topic vocabulary?		
Can you find a range of sentence types?		

SPEAKING

PART 1

1 Now, in this first part, I'd like to ask you some questions about yourself. Let's talk about your work. Where do you work?
Do you enjoy your work? Why / Why not?
What kinds of tasks do you have to do at work?
Have you ever been late for work?
Why / Why not?

2 I'd like to move on now to talk about fashion. Tell me about the popular clothes and fashions in your country.
What sort of fashion shops do you have in your country?
Have fashions changed very much since you were younger?
Is it important for you to be in fashion? Why / Why not?

If you have someone to study with, take it in turns to ask and answer the questions.

3 Let's move on to the topic of the internet.
How often do you use the internet?
Does everyone in your family use the internet?
What do you use the internet for?
When did you last use the internet?

((◗ Listen to the sample on the recording and complete the checklist. (CD Track 16)

	✔	Comments
Did the student directly answer the questions?		
Did he use a range of words?		
Did he link his ideas together well?		
Did he say enough?		
Were the answers easy to understand?		

PART 2

Describe a place that you would like to visit.

You should say:
where it is
when you would like to go there
who you would like to go with

and explain why you would like to visit this place.

1 Now, I'm going to give you a topic, and I'd like you to talk about it for one to two minutes.
Before you talk, you'll have one minute to think about what you're going to say.
You can make some notes if you wish. Do you understand?
Here's some paper and a pencil, for making notes, and here's your topic.

If you have someone to study with, take it in turns to do the talk in one to two minutes.

((◗ Listen to the sample on the recording and complete the checklist. (CD Track 17)

	✔	Comments
Did the student talk for two minutes?		
Did he stick to the topic?		
Did he cover the three main points?		
Did the talk flow well?		
Did he use a range of words?		

2 All right?
Remember you have one to two minutes for this, so don't worry if I stop you. I'll tell you when the time is up. Can you start speaking now, please?

⚷→ ANSWERS PAGE 116

PART 3

1 We've been talking about a place you'd like to visit and I'd like to discuss with you one or two more general questions related to this.

So, let's consider first of all the idea, as a student, of having a gap year.

2 How important do you think it is for young people to visit different places before they go to university or college? What sort of challenges do you think you'd have, going on a gap year as a student? Do you think it's useful to work, for other reasons as well, besides money? What sort of jobs do you think would be the best sort of jobs to do? What sort of preparation should a student make before they go on a gap year, do you think?

3 OK. Let's move on to the topic of travelling to less familiar places. What sort of advantages are there to reading about a country before you visit it? Do you think there are any disadvantages? Some people choose to have a guide, when they go to a very unfamiliar place. Do you think that improves the quality of a travel experience? Do you think you learn more from visiting important sites or from meeting local people?

If you have someone to study with, take it in turns to ask and answer the questions.

((▶ Listen to the sample recording and complete the checklist. (CD Track 18)

	✔	Comments
Did the student respond to the key ideas?		
Did the student support his answers well?		
Did he use a range of words?		
Did he speak fluently, using a range of linkers?		

⚷ **ANSWERS PAGE 116**

Answer Key

Listing Section 1

1 a, c, f, h

Pick from a list

2 identification / passport
study English / learn a language
fly / go by plane
building / house
painting / picture
headgear / helmet
vehicle / car
meal / lunch
bag / suitcase
thunderstorm / wet weather
winter sports / skiing

3 and **4** C, E (in any order)

Form filling

5 NB Answers provide examples of how these times and
dates are said, not written.
Seven fifty / Ten to eight (in the morning)
Six forty-five / A quarter to seven (in the morning)
Ten fifteen / A quarter past ten (in the morning)
One am / One o'clock (in the morning)
Thirteen hundred hours / One pm / One o'clock (in the
afternoon)

6 The twenty-first of November / November the twenty-first
The twenty-fourth of March / March the twenty-fourth
The twenty-second of December / December the twenty-
second
The eighteenth of August / August the eighteenth

7 a a name **b** a date with a year **c** a family name
d a condition / an illness

8 C A R O L I N E Black

9 22 November 1984 / 22nd November 1984 / November
22nd 1984 / November 22 1984

10 129 807

11 Ford station wagon

Labelling a map or plan

12 Queen Victoria Building

13 Bottom right-hand corner

14 Market Street, Martin Place, Hunter Street, Bridge Street

15 The Opera House

16 Queen Victoria Building / QVB

17 department store

18 hotel

19 library

Listening Section 2

1 A Pavilion / built 1784 / re-built 1815–1820 / Indian and
Chinese styles

B koala park / zoo
koalas popular / loveable appearance but long claws /
be careful

Sentence/summary completion

2 a a noun (form of transport)
b a noun (animal or plant)
c a number (date/period)
d a noun (material)
e an adjective (positive)
f an adjective (negative)

3 200 years / two hundred years

4 (white) stone

5 under (the) waves/water / underwater

6 summer months / summer

7 It is OK to use words or figures here.

Table completion

8 comparing 3 hotels: key words are rate / rate includes /
facilities

9 A a service **B** $ amount and a service **C** a facility

10 11.15 am (must have *am* or *morning*)

11 *The Long Journey*

12 (classic) action (film)

Short answer questions

13 a When / restaurant *Time or date*
b Where / paintings *Place: building or city*
c How many / concert *Number*
d Why / telephone *Reason*
e What / man's bag *Item/thing = noun*
f Who / party *Person or name*
g What / old lady *Event or incident*
h How / hurt *Explanation*

14 ground floor

15 photography / photographs

16 films / lectures / concerts

17 Q16 must have two pieces of information to get one mark.

Listening Section 3

1 B A C

2 C B A D

3 Set 1 – Speaker C; Set 2 – Speaker B

4 Set 1 – Speaker B; Set 2 – Speakers B and D

5 A iii **B** i

6 A no **B** yes **C** no

Multiple choice

7 C

8 Possible re-phrasing of the three options.
A To protect them from illness.
B To provide them with extra food.
C So that they stay pink in colour.

9 Option A: flamingo health is not mentioned on the
recording, so option A is not correct. Option B: food and
diet are mentioned on the recording, but the speaker says
not getting enough food was not the problem, so option B
is not correct.

Matching

10 B played in many countries / popular all over the world
   C could be harmful / could hurt yourself
   D lots of people play this
   E the things you need to play cost a lot of money
   F not difficult to learn
   G fun to look at / good spectator sport

11 E
12 B
13 F
14 C

15 if it included some more examples / usually pretty good / groundbreaking / very high standard / hasn't been assessed yet

Labelling a diagram

16 C
17 D
18 E

Listening Section 4

1 1 f **2** c **3** a **4** b **5** d **6** e **7** g **8** h **9** j **10** i

2 A In fact / Surprisingly enough (2/4)
   B On the other hand (10)
   C One way (1)
   D lastly (6)
   E generally speaking (8)
   F surprisingly enough / in fact / generally speaking (4/2/8)

Note completion

3 The topic is science/DNA.
   What does a string of DNA look like?
   What two things does DNA have something in common with?
4 an object / something biological
5 ball of string
6 other animals / plants
7 Australia
8 marketing strategies
9 TV programme

Flow chart completion

10 by hand
11 mills
12 labelled
13 at home / abroad
14 the first step is to / after this initial process / incidentally / then / finally

Classification

15 waste disposal methods
16 ways of disposing of different materials
17 C **18** C **19** A **20** A **21** B

Academic Reading Section 1

Sentence completion

1 date/number
2 plural/uncountable noun
3 comparative adjective
4 *singular noun*   wind tunnel
5 number and distance   50 kilometres
6 uncountable noun   (mechanical) energy/power
7 plural noun   (flying) machines
8 a not enough / article unnecessary
   b spelling error / too many words, *per hour* unnecessary
   c not the aim / not uncountable
   d not plural / these make humans fail

Notes / table / flow chart completion

9 A is a full sentence and the answer must be *a power station* or *power stations*.
   B is notes and the article can be omitted from *power station*.
10 the world / global
11 and **12** construction workers, farmers (in any order)
13 and **14** orchestral musicians, airline pilots (in any order)
15 loud bangs
16 examples = such as
   good hearing = hear well
   most dangerous = do the most damage

Short answer questions

17 (in) permanent settlements
18 (central) oases
19 (artesian) wells
20 (date) palms
21 one per cent
22 *what water sources + developed / what land constructions + irrigation / which crop / how much of the water + homes*

Labelling a diagram

23 (row of) beds
24 television (TV is wrong because it isn't in the article)
25 (two / large) storage bins (you can add *two* or *large* but not both as this would make four words)
26 sugar cane
27 situated high, leading off, along, in the middle of, from which, in the centre of, in the corner, surrounding, beyond, on the outer edge

True / False / Not Given

29 in the early 1950s / the media;
   at the turn of the twentieth century / by 1952 / the press;
   man had reached his athletic limits / room for improvement was minimal: True
30 in 1980 / Vladimir Salnikov;
   Vladimir Salnikov, who in 1980;
   became the first man to break 15 minutes for 1500 metres: True

31 John Landy and Roger Bannister
athletes such as Bannister and Landy / for both men;
the amateur environment in which they competed / they
received no monetary reward: False

32 Bannister's record;
Bannister's record;
has since been reduced: Not Given

Global multiple choice

34 B

35 A Improvements are mentioned but only in running and
swimming.
  C Young people are not the focus, although the article is
obviously encouraging.
  D A comparison is made as a supporting point, not as the
main theme of the text.

Academic Reading Section 2

Matching

1 B **2** A **3** D **4** C **5** A

6 unfortunate = complained; focus of advertising =
advertising used to be about; changed = used to be + now

Finding information in paragraphs

7 B

8 B originally located

9 C mollusc scavenger

10 A much like we do today

11 C transported them to the cave

Sentence completion with a box

13 B

14 A is grammatically incorrect because *waste* is
uncountable. C is incorrect because it is illogical.

15 D **16** F **17** A **18** G

Yes / No / Not Given

19 Most of it is the writer's claims. The information about the
pin-tumbler lock is mainly fact.

20 N **21** Y **22** NG **23** Y **24** NG **25** Y **26** N

27 *it is perhaps not surprising that most people pay little*
[23Y] *attention to where their energy comes from or what*
impact using it is having on the environment.

[24NG] *greener and cleaner energy sources*

[25Y] *Some two billion people are still without electricity, the*
majority of whom live in poor countries

[26N] *emerging energy sources could mean the foundation of*
new high-tech industries that employ hundreds of
thousands of people.

Multiple choice

28 A

29 B *For more than 60 years* sounds like a long time but the
writer does not say anything negative about this.
  C The writer does not say it was well planned.
  D Although birds are mentioned, they are mostly located
away from the factory and town.

Academic Reading Section 3

Paragraph headings

1 iii

2 *global* matches *world's*; *times ahead* matches *the future.*

3 There are many present continuous verb forms with future
meaning.

4 i The reference is to population figures in the whole
world, not just in China.
  ii The reference to farmland in the paragraph is
worldwide, not just in China.

5 iv

6 v

7 ii

8 i This is mentioned briefly but is not a key idea.
  iii Found books are mentioned, but not lost books.

Summary completion

9 It will be a noun (countable or singular).

10 Noun / singular – could be a place

11 Noun / plural – something valuable from the past

12 Noun / plural – people, perhaps swimmers or divers

13 biochemical

14 energy

15 iron and manganese (not uranium)

16 gold chloride

17 colour

18 a find it hard to understand
  b natural gold deposits form
  c what is happening
  d conducted
  e bacteria
  f tend to prefer… for lunch
  g turned

Summary completion with a box

19 important algae / expelled / occurs / turns

20 important algae being expelled

21 coral bleaching

22 F (in the right place)

23 B (number or size of the rooms)

24 C (furniture)

25 G (in the same way)

26 D (number of nurses and doctors)

Classification

Features	Relief	Calm	Answer
29 causes sleepiness	✗	✓	B
30 is easy to swallow	✗	✓	B
31 works quickly	✓	✓	C

Pick from a list

33 and **34** D, E (in any order)

35 D no longer just for kids / it is becoming popular among
adults
  E to fight cavities

Academic Writing Task 1

1 percentage
2 changes
3 vertical
4 time
5 data
6 troughs
7 trends
8 line
9 axes
10 years
11 compare
12 columns

Content

1 different
2 percentage
3 soccer
4 cricket
5 swimming
6 soccer
7 15 per cent / 15%
8 category
9 cricket
10 four per cent / 4%
11 popular
12 majority
13 Suggested answer:
The diagram shows how recycled glass is used to make new glass bottles.
14 recycled glass
15 heats
16 molten glass
17 More
18 most popular
19 While / fewer
20 Hardly
21 The bar graph provides information about the most common sports played in Australia in 2003. It gives figures for both boys and girls and clearly shows that their participation in sports is fairly equal. However, their sporting preferences tend to be different.

According to the graph, the most popular sport among girls is netball, with participation rates reaching 25 per cent. A similar percentage of boys prefer soccer, which is clearly their favourite sport. Ten per cent of boys also enjoy playing cricket but hardly any girls take part in this game. While swimming is popular among both boys and girls, fewer boys participate in this sport – about 13 per cent compared to approximately 22 per cent of girls.

Other sports such as tennis, basketball and martial arts have lower levels of popularity, and a significant percentage of boys and girls say they enjoy sports not referred to on the chart.

22 Suggested answer:
Similarities: both use percentages / both cover the same sports
Differences: Graph 1 is about 5–14-year-olds and Graph 2 is more general / Graph 1 shows only the percentage of sports played / Graph 2 shows the breakdown of boys' and girls' sport / Graph 2 does not include a non-playing category
Key features: swimming is most popular generally but girls' figure is higher / boys' preferred sport is soccer (also mention cricket), while girls prefer netball / large non-playing category in Graph1

23 participation / involvement
24 swimming
25 girls
26 boys
27 percentage
28 Suggested answer:
Netball, on the other hand, is played almost exclusively by 25 per cent of girls, while cricket is mostly a boys' sport. Tennis and basketball are slightly more popular than martial arts and athletics, all of which are played by under 10 per cent of children. Finally, it should be mentioned that about 17 per cent of children do not play any sport at all.

Overall, the graphs show that while boys and girls enjoy a range of sports, their preferences are quite different.

Organisation

1 trends similar but men eat more at all ages
2 15–25 age group eats the most
3 food consumption levels out as people get older
4 ages of 2 and 65
5 similar
6 more
7 13000 kilojoules
8 greatest / high(est)
9 peak
10 9000 kilojoules
11 As far as consumption rates are concerned
12 as
13 After this
14 with
15 also
16 generally
17 it
18 This figure
19 they / this
20 both
21 the greatest
22 which

Vocabulary

1 material
2 annually

3 clear / apparent

4 chart / graph

5 frequently

6 and the second / and the next

7 total

8 vast majority / vast number
serious consideration
small minority / small amount / small proportion / small majority
downward trend
considerable amount / considerable proportion / considerable number
reasonable proportion / reasonable number

9 d

10 g

11 b

12 h

13 e

14 a

15 f

16 c

17 residents – resident
hole – whole
aluminum – aluminium
recycling – recycled
producers – products
normal – normally
quantitys – quantities

Grammar

1 can be pumped

2 needs to be situated

3 acts

4 is sunk

5 is pumped

6 overflows

7 is used to carry

8 is submerged

9 (is) connected

10 is attached

11 carries

12 is concealed

13 appears

14 is flowing

15 being recycled

16 was consumed

17 shows

18 which were eaten / eaten

19 highest

20 were consumed

21 a

22 ate

Suggested answer:

As far as consumption for men and women is concerned, there is generally little difference between the two. In most cases, women eat roughly the same amount of chocolate as men. The only countries where this is not the case are Belgium and Austria, where women eat almost twice as much as men.

Overall it seems that very different quantities of chocolate are eaten around the world but, generally speaking, this product is more popular in Europe than elsewhere.

Academic Writing Task 2

Content

1

B	Yes	extra private lessons / do better at school	Two – advantages and disadvantages
C	No	traffic congestion / increasing / causes / reduce problems	Two – causes and how to reduce problems

2 There are two questions to address in task C, so your position will relate both to the causes and whether you think the problems can be reduced.

3 The writer's position is the final sentence. It represents position i.

4 Suggested answer:
In my view, this is a bad idea for a number of reasons.

5 The writer's position is re-stated from *there is no doubt…* onwards.

6 Suggested answer:
As a child, I received a lot of private tuition. My parents believed they were helping me to get better grades in my exams – and perhaps they did. However, I can only remember being very tired all through my school life, and my view now is that private lessons put too much pressure on children.

7 Suggested answer:
student's pace of learning / can ask more questions / attention on individual; cost of lessons / already very busy or tired / travel to tutor's home

8 The second sentence contains the supporting argument.

9 Suggested answer:
roadworks and poor roads / increase in vehicles on roads / ineffective public transport; avoid rush hour / higher petrol prices / more alternative options

10 Suggested answer:
Wherever people live, it seems that the volume of traffic is increasing. Roads that were once easy to drive along have become congested, and it takes longer to get where you want to go.

One of the main causes of traffic congestion is the affordability of cars. People of my grandparents' generation did not have enough money to buy a car, so they were happy living without one. Now some families have more than one car and young people learn to drive as soon as they can. This means that car ownership is constantly increasing.

Organisation

1 The main ideas are the second and fifth sentences. The second paragraph could start with *Students can.*

2 ii The fifth sentence should be linked back to *number of reasons.*

3 i and iv signal a contrasting point and iii isn't logical.

4 a One way
 b Another way of reducing traffic congestion
 c more controversial

5 Suggested answer:

There are a number of ways that we can help solve the problems of traffic congestion. *One way* would be to make sure that every family only has one car. Although this may seem difficult at first, families often find that they can organise their lives so that they can share a car, or make better use of public transport.

Another way of reducing traffic congestion would be to increase the cost of petrol. If fuel was more expensive, people would soon decide to drive less and walk more or take a bus and, as a result, there would be less traffic.

A *more controversial* solution would be to charge people for road use. Generally speaking, this approach has been successful, particularly when the toll is on very busy roads.

6

it	water	some	governments
they	*governments*	both approaches	limiting and recycling water
their	governments'	the first	limiting water use

7 a where
 b their
 c their
 d this
 e they
 f the / this / their
 g which
 h their
 i these / the
 j This

8 So initially / Once / and / such as

9 Suggested answer:

Some countries do not have an unlimited supply of water and others may have periods of drought when water use has to be reduced. In addition to encouraging their citizens to use less water, it seems a lot more effort could be put into developing recycling schemes. Water that has been used for baths and showers, for example, could be used for flushing toilets, rather than being left to simply run down the drain.

Vocabulary

1 It comes from a newspaper article.

2 a air pollution
 b diesel / petrol
 c climate change
 d transport
 e journeys
 f traffic
 g new roads
 h impact
 i symbols of personal status
 j comfort, convenience
 k car-dependent lifestyles

3 a (e)specially
 b drivers
 c delays
 d wasting
 e fewer
 f increasing
 g manufacturing
 h inexpensive
 i charged

Grammar

1 a full stop after *pollution* and start new sentence
 b question mark after *this*
 c comma after *vehicles* not *or*
 d *scientists*
 e full stop not question mark
 f comma after *example* not colon
 g full stop at end

Speaking Part 1

1 a

2 Suggested answer:
 a Canterbury.
 b Canterbury's in the south-east corner of England. It's quite near the coast.
 c I've lived there for 18 years.
 d Yes, it's OK. It's quite a big city so there are plenty of things for young people to do, lots of shops and some parks. And it's a historical place so there are some very interesting tourist sites there.
 e Not really. I suppose I'd quite like it if it was a bit bigger. But I think, on the whole, it's a good place to live.

3 Suggested answer:
 What kind of work or studies do you do?
 Where do you work or study?
 How long have you had this job / been studying?
 Do you like your area of work or study?
 Is there anything you dislike about it?

4 Suggested answer:
 Reading material: magazine/book/comic
 Forms of transport: bus/motorbike/tram
 Types of building: museum/factory/school
 Weather: sunshine/mist/snow
 Types of celebration: wedding/festival/party
 Hobbies/interests: dancing/swimming/languages
 Types of entertainment: film/tenpin bowling/karaoke
 Types of scenery: moorland/desert/coastline

5 Your own answer.

6 a tiring
 b impressive

c informative
d depressing
e enjoyable / relaxing / sociable
f scary / impressive
g sociable
h relaxing
i complicated / depressing

7 b flight
c polluted
d helpful
e freedom
f comfortable
g golfer
h crowded

8 a C **b** B **c** E **d** D **e** A **f** D **g** E

9 Suggested answer:
B I prefer to travel by car because I like to look at the scenery. Although planes can get you there a lot quicker, I think I find air travel a bit stressful.
C When I'm on holiday, I like to visit interesting places in the area. I'm an active person, so beach holidays and that kind of thing don't really interest me. I need to do things.
D I think people have to have a break from their everyday routine so that they can feel refreshed. Also, these days, life has become extremely hectic. Everyone's always in a rush, so we need to slow things down from time to time.
E For my last holiday, I went camping in the countryside with some friends. It was much better than I'd expected. The weather was really warm and we did lots of hill walking and got very fit. I didn't enjoy the food very much, though!

10 Suggested answer:
a My favourite subject's English because it's very useful and…
b At school. I started learning English when I was only five, so I've been doing it a long time!
c I much prefer a small class. Big classes are far too impersonal and it's never possible for the teacher to give their attention to everyone.
d Yes, I'm going to take IELTS because…
e A school play! I can't really remember… maybe I was in one when I was very young.
f Yes, they've introduced several changes. One is… another is…

11 a I come from Tokyo.
b I play basketball.
c Yes. I like fashion very much.
d I have lived with my family since I was born.
e I find it hard to pronounce English words. / It isn't easy for me to pronounce English words.
f I enjoy discussing economics.
g I'm thinking of going to America.
h Most people go away in the summer.
i I don't eat much fruit.

Speaking Part 2

1 scientific development / benefited / what type / why needed / how used / why beneficial
2 Suggested answer:
A winter sports / cross-country skiing
B school trip / visit from relatives
C singer / sportsperson
D carnival / festival
E weekend job / job for parents
F school pantomime / music festival
3 Although getting married seemed an easy topic, it wasn't. The student decided on it before he had thought about whether he had enough things to say.
4 Your own answer.
5 The plan that you have more to say about produces more ideas in your notes.
6 enjoy / 've always been / was / used to watch / dream / had / were / have / try
7 Points: why you like it; when you started doing it; how often you do it now.
8 A was born / lived / finished or had finished / went / was
B is / elected / stays / is or would be / would feel
C got / was / came / don't / was
9 a hiking
b schoolfriends
c mountain
d takes hours
e steep
f view from the top

Speaking Part 3

1 a, c, d, f, h
2 benefits / travelling / new places
3 The student could illustrate the key ideas (see below). By giving a full answer the student may also be able to influence the direction of the discussion.
Sample answer:
I think there are quite a number of benefits. For a start, it can be very exciting to visit a different country, *because you see and experience things that are quite new and unfamiliar to you*, and it can also be personally rewarding too. *For example, you might change your plans for the future as a result of your trip.*
4 Your own answer.
5 countries rely on tourism
6 Job / work / career / choosing a career / value of work / employer's responsibilities
Fun in preparing for the performance / benefits of taking part / using drama in school education / value of the theatre and cinema in society
7 How would you advise people to choose a career?
How important is work in a person's life?
Is it right that a nurse gets less money than a doctor?
What might you learn from taking part in a performance?

Should children have the chance to perform at school? What role do the arts play in society today?

8 Suggested answer:

For me having a hobby is terribly important *because* I get very stressed in my job, so I have to do something that relaxes me. If I didn't have any hobbies, I think I would just work and that would be very bad for my health.

Some people feel that sport is a waste of time because there are so many other things to do in life. Perhaps if they're really busy, they have a point. *But I actually think* you learn a lot of social skills through sport, like working as part of a team and negotiating tactics.

I don't really think the Olympic Games are a very good way of building international relations. I think people get too serious about their own country winning. *On the other hand, the FIFA World Cup is always fantastic. I really* think it unites everyone who enjoys it – we're all watching it at the same time and we get involved in games even if our own country isn't playing.

Practice Test

Listening Section 1
1 to 3 D, E, H (in any order)
4 29 LOCH Street
5 558 992
6 Saturday 1 May / 1st May / May 1st
7 8 weeks / 2 months
8 A
9 E
10 D

Listening Section 2
11 cities
12 (a) palace
13 (the) coat hanger
14 government / state / state government
15 1924
16 800 houses
17 9.5 million
18 horse
19 2.3 kms / 2.3 kilometres
20 (a) ship / (an) earthquake

Listening Section 3
21 A
22 H
23 D
24 E
25 A
26 (the) Painted Gallery
27 (the) Main Gallery
28 B
29 A
30 C

Listening Section 4
31 selling / advertising (must have both words)
32 making money / a profit
33 warmth / safety (must have both words)
34 individual
35 C 36 A 37 B 38 A
39 satisfied
40 better than expected

Academic Reading Section 1
1 conditions
2 craftsmen and artists / artists and craftsmen
3 a secure livelihood
4 (the) Grand Gallery
5 481 feet
6 (the) Queen's Chamber
7 (two) air channel(s)
8 F
9 NG
10 T
11 T
12 F
13 D

Academic Reading Section 2
14 D
15 B
16 A
17 A
18 C
19 C
20 F
21 D
22 A
23 C
24 E
25 G
26 B

Academic Reading Section 3
27 vii
28 v
29 ix
30 i
31 iv
32 iii
33 re-offending
34 sentencing
35 victim
36 restorative justice
37 A
38 C
39 D
40 B

Academic Writing Task 1
Suggested answer:

This diagram provides an overview of a domestic central heating system. It shows how the tank, boiler and pipes ensure a constant flow of hot water to both the radiators and the taps.

The cold water enters the house and is stored in a water storage tank in the roof. From there it flows down to the boiler, located on the ground floor of the house.

The boiler, which is fuelled by gas or oil, heats up the water as it passes through it. The hot water is then pumped round the house through a system of pipes and flows into the radiators, located in different rooms. The water circulates through the radiators, which have small tubes inside them to help distribute the heat, and this warms each of the rooms. Some of the water is directed to the taps to provide hot water for the house.

Once the water has been through the pipes and radiators, it is returned to the boiler to be re-heated and circulated round the house again.

Introduction: First sentence.

Overview: Second sentence.

Key features: Entry of cold water into boiler; circulation of hot water to radiators and taps; return of water to boiler.

Supporting information: direction of flow; types of boiler; location of radiators; radiator tubes

Paragraph breaks: The paragraph breaks mark stages in the process.

Linkers: and, from there, then, once, again

Reference words: it, both, there, which, this

Topic vocabulary: enters, stored, roof, flows, ground floor, located, passes, pumped, system, circulates, heat, directed, returned, re-heated

Less common vocabulary: ensure, fuelled by, heats up, distribute the heat, warms

Structures: An appropriate mix of active and passive structures and a range of sentence types are used.

Length: 172 words

Academic Writing Task 2

Suggested answer:

There is plenty of evidence to suggest that children are overweight and the situation is getting worse, according to the medical experts. I feel there are a number of reasons for this.

Some people blame the fact that we are surrounded by shops selling unhealthy, fatty foods such as chips and fried chicken, at low prices. This has created a whole generation of adults who have never cooked a meal for themselves. If there were fewer of these restaurants, then children would not be tempted to buy take-away food.

There is another argument that blames the parents for allowing their children to become overweight. I tend to agree with this view, because good eating habits begin early in life, long before children start to visit fast food outlets. If children are given chips and chocolate rather than nourishing food, or are always allowed to choose what they eat, they will go for the sweet and salty foods every time, and this will carry on throughout their lives.

There is a third factor, however, which contributes to the situation. Children these days take very little exercise. They do not walk to school. When they get home, they sit in front of the television or their computers and play video games. Not only is this an unhealthy pastime, it also gives them time to eat more junk food. What they need is to go outside and play active games or sport.

The two views discussed play an equal role in contributing to the problem, but I think we have to encourage young people to be more active, as well as steering them away from fast food outlets and bad eating habits. We need to have a balanced approach.

Position: Writer refers to a number of reasons in the introduction, and to the need for a balanced view in the conclusion.

Main ideas: First sentence of the second paragraph; first and second sentences of the third paragraph; second sentence of the fourth paragraph.

Linkers: and, according to, some people, such as, if, then, there is another argument, because, or, there is a third factor, however, not only, also, the two views discussed, but, as well as

Reference words: the, this, who, themselves, these, this view, they, their, them

Topic vocabulary: medical experts, shops, unhealthy, fatty foods, chips, cooked, take-away food, chocolate, sweet and salty, exercise, walk, television, computers, video games, unhealthy pastime, junk food, active games, sport, fast food outlets

Sentence types: A wide range of complex structures and sentences is used.

Length: 286 words

Speaking Part 1

The student gave relevant answers to all the questions, using a range of appropriate vocabulary and linkers. The answers were clear and sufficiently long for Part 1.

Speaking Part 2

The student was able to speak for two minutes and kept to the topic. He covered all the points in the task and used a range of vocabulary and linkers. He allowed himself time to think, when necessary.

Speaking Part 3

The student responded well to the main ideas in the questions and gave full answers, with plenty of support. He discussed the topics with ease, using a good range of words and expressions. As the student was a native speaker, he made no grammatical errors, pronounced words clearly and used rhythm, stress and intonation well.

Recording Scripts

Listening Section 1

Extract 1 (CD Track 1)

Man   Good morning. Motor Registry.

Woman   Oh, good morning. I'd like to arrange a day to take my driving test.

Man   OK. Have you done the Knowledge Test yet?

Woman   Yes, I've passed that. I got 99%.

Man   Right. What's your name and I'll just check that on the computer. Oh, no! The computers aren't working right now. You'll have to give me your details and I'll call you back. What's your name?

Woman   Caroline Black, that's C A R O L I N E Black.

Man   OK and your date of birth?

Woman   22nd of November, 1984.

Man   November the 22nd, that's today. Happy birthday! Nineteen eighty-four. And can you give me a contact number so I can call you back?

Woman   I'll give you my mobile – it's 0412 129 807.

Man   0412 129... Did you say 811?

Woman   No... 807.

Man   Right. Got it. And can you tell me what make and model of car you'll be using for the test?

Woman   Yes, it's a Ford – a Ford station wagon. It's my dad's car.

Man   OK. Ford station wagon. Well, when the computers are working again, I'll call you back with a date for the test.

Woman   Oh. All right. Thanks...

Extract 2 (CD Track 2)

Woman   Excuse me. Can you tell me how to get to the library? I seem to have got rather lost.

Man   Sure! Well you're a little off course. It's about a ten-minute walk from here. Have you got a map?

Woman   Yes. Here it is.

Man   Now, let me see. You're here at the moment. I'll put a cross on the map to show you where you are.

Woman   Thanks.

Man   OK. So you walk along George Street, past the Queen Victoria Building on your left. We call that the QVB.

Woman   Oh, I see.

Man   Go past the QVB and turn right into Market Street. There's a bank on the opposite corner. And a department store on the other corner.

Woman   So I turn right.

Man   Yes, you turn right and walk past a lovely old theatre on your right, that's opposite the department store. That's called the State Theatre.

Woman   OK. Past the theatre and...

Man   Then you need to turn left into Pitt Street. That's a pedestrian street, with no cars and lots of shops. There are shops along both sides of the street.

Woman   Oh, yes, I think I've been there before.

Man   Walk along Pitt Street until you come to Martin Place. The old post office building is on your left – except that it's not the post office any more, it's now a big hotel; the post office has gone.

Woman   Oh that's a shame. I bet it's an expensive hotel!

Man   Probably. I've never stayed there myself! Go across Martin Place, and then just continue walking along Pitt Street and you'll come to Hunter Street. Turn right and then walk straight ahead for a couple of blocks until you come to a main road. The library is on the other side of the road, but you can't miss it.

Woman   Thank you so much.

Listening Section 2

Extract 1 (CD Track 3)

On today's programme about great buildings of the world, I'm going to talk about the Bell Rock lighthouse – perhaps one of the greatest engineering feats of the 19th century, and I'm sure you'll agree that this is a fascinating story. It's nearly 200 years since the lighthouse was first built, and when you look at where it's situated, you'll see why this was such a remarkable achievement.

The Bell Rock lighthouse, also known as Stevenson's lighthouse after the engineer who built it, is 11 miles off the east coast of Scotland in the North Sea. It consists of a white stone tower over 100 feet high, that's over 30 metres high, and it rises out of the sea, apparently without any support. It is a truly amazing sight! But, in fact, despite what it looks like, the tower is actually built on a sandstone reef which lies just under the waves.

Because the Bell Rock is underwater for so much of the time, it has always presented a great danger to shipping and many ships were lost over the centuries. And, it has also presented a huge engineering challenge, for it's no easy business to build a lighthouse under such conditions. In the first year of construction, work could only take place in the summer months when the tide was low. And it is a credit to Stevenson and his colleagues that this incredible structure has not required a single repair to its stonework since the day it was completed in 1811...

Extract 2 (CD Track 4)

Thank you for calling the Rialto Family Cinemas. The following information is for Saturday 3rd February. Please collect reserved tickets 15 minutes before the commencement of the film. In Cinema One, we are showing *Shrek 2*, the sequel to the smash hit *Shrek*. One performance only this morning at a quarter past eleven. This is an animated fairytale – suitable for all the family.

In Cinema Two, we have the award-winning documentary *The Long Journey* commencing at 6.15 pm. Don't miss this extraordinary first-hand account.

In Cinema Three, by popular demand, the Jackie Chan favourite *Armour of God*. Commencing at 5.30 pm with a repeat performance at 9.15. This is Jackie Chan at his best in a classic action film.

Extract 3 (CD Track 5)

Welcome to the City Art Gallery and to our gallery audio tour. The Gallery was first established in 1875 and is now one of the city's most popular attractions. The building has undergone a number of changes over the years, the most recent addition being the extension on the <u>ground floor</u>, which was opened in 1988.

The Gallery houses some of the finest works of art in Australia including Aboriginal, European and Asian paintings. There is a comprehensive Australian collection, which includes works from the early colonial period to the present day. In addition to the paintings on display, we have an excellent collection of <u>photography</u>, with <u>photographs</u> dating from the 19th century.

As well as the permanent collection which you will see throughout the building, the Art Gallery has a varied and exciting exhibition programme with approximately 30 changing exhibitions each year. Many of these exhibitions are accompanied by <u>films and lectures or occasionally by concerts</u>.

Now let's begin our tour in the 19th century Australian room…

Listening Section 3

Extract 1 (CD Track 6)

Man   So flamingos in zoos need to eat algae, do they? Why's that?

Woman Well, for a long while, flamingos living in captivity, for example in zoos, kept losing their delicate pink colour and fading to white. Then the zookeepers realised the problem was due to the birds' diet.

Man   Weren't they getting enough food?

Woman No, that wasn't the problem. It was that, <u>in the wild, flamingos feed on a certain kind of algae containing chemicals called carotenoids, which give the birds their distinctive colour.</u>

Extract 2 (CD Track 7)

Man   I believe researchers are exploring the idea of a padded car to reduce injuries in accidents. Can you tell us something about what it will be like?

Woman Yes. Well, the car <u>will be covered in plastic cells</u> filled with air, moulded round a conventional metal frame.

Man   I see. So the plastic cells will allow cars to bounce off each other.

Woman Exactly. And you'd also be able to see what's just behind you on the road because there's a camera mounted on the back.

Man   Any other innovations?

Woman The <u>doors will open upwards and out, giving the appearance of a wing</u> when open, and the wheels will go in all directions to assist in heavy traffic. And to guide motorists away from traffic jams and help them find a parking spot, the car will be <u>fitted with a computer</u> near the steering wheel.

Man   Where the driver can see it, of course.

Woman Yes. There's also a hook to allow novel parking techniques.

Man   It sounds amazing!

Listening Section 4

Extract 1 (CD Track 8)

Did you know that within the nucleus of each of your cells is a set of instructions for building you from scratch? Amazingly, if you could stretch it out, this string of acid, or DNA as it is known, would be about three feet long: but in fact, it's tangled up like a <u>ball of string</u>. Various parts of the string incorporate between 50,000 and 100,000 separate genes. A human individual's complete set of genetic material is known as the human genome. And interestingly, the human genome is not the biggest one around. Surprisingly enough, your genome has a lot in common with other <u>animals and plants</u>. Nonetheless, your DNA sequence is uniquely yours.

Extract 2 (CD Track 9)

Lonely Planet is one of a number of highly successful publishers of travel books. The company is <u>based in Australia</u> but also has offices in a number of other countries. The travel guide business is a highly competitive market, and so to compete, they have adopted a range of <u>marketing strategies</u>. One thing they excel at is tracking individual customers, which in turn allows them to measure how well their marketing is working. They've also licensed the name, <u>Lonely Planet, to a TV programme</u> of the same name, as part of their overall strategy.

Extract 3 (CD Track 10)

The production of olive oil is an expensive business. The best oil comes from olives that have been hand picked, as machines tend to damage the fruit, so the first step is to <u>pick the olives by hand</u>. After this initial process, the fruit is <u>transported to the mills</u>, where it is carefully crushed. Incidentally the very best oil, known as extra virgin oil, comes from the first crush. The paste which results from the crushing process is mixed until oil droplets form and the precious 'liquid gold' is then bottled in beautiful containers and <u>labelled</u> to show its origin. The oil finally finds its way into shops and supermarkets both <u>at home and abroad</u>.

Extract 4 (CD Track 11)

Some people believe that when you're learning a language, the best way to improve your speaking is in the language laboratory, but I firmly believe that <u>it's better to work in small groups because then you can also improve your listening at the same time</u>. After all, speaking and listening go together, don't they? And somehow it seems more natural to work in groups. The language lab is a <u>good enough place to practise your pronunciation</u> and you can also <u>improve your grammar by doing practice drills in the lab</u>, even if it's a bit boring. As far as reading is concerned, nothing beats <u>working on your own</u> and reading as much as possible whenever you have the chance.

Practice Test Recording Scripts

Section 1 (CD Track 12)

Agent   Good morning. Can I help you?

Customer Yes, I'd like to get some information about trips to New Zealand.

Agent   Certainly. Take a seat and I'll be right with you.

Customer Thanks.

Agent	Now, where would you like to go in New Zealand?
Customer	Well, I was hoping to do a bit of travelling around, actually. There are a few things I'd like to see and do before I go back home.
Agent	Right.
Customer	One thing I really want to do is go to Christchurch. I have relatives living there that I can stay with – my mother's cousin – and I've heard it's a nice place.
Agent	Yes, it's a lovely city. And staying with relatives will help with the budget, of course.
Customer	The budget?
Agent	It will save you some money.
Customer	Oh right! Well, I'm not too worried about that. I've saved quite a bit of money working in Australia.
Agent	Oh, that's nice. Good for you! Well, you know that New Zealand consists of two main islands, the North Island and the South Island, and Christchurch is on the South Island.
Customer	Is it? I was never very good at geography at school! Do you have a map I could look at?
Agent	Sure! Here we are.
Customer	Right. I see. And… well… then I'd also like to spend some time in Auckland. And maybe I could do an English language course there. Can you organise that sort of thing for me?
Agent	Certainly. We'd be happy to arrange that. But bear in mind that Auckland is in the North Island.
Customer	OK. And I'd also like to do some skiing or maybe even some snowboarding. I hear New Zealand is a great place for that.
Agent	Yes, absolutely. But you should go to Auckland first for your studies, and then you can get the ferry across to the South Island and take the bus down to the snow.
Customer	Oh, I don't like boats very much. I'm not much of a sailor. I think I'd prefer to fly.
Agent	Right. What about joining a walking tour? That could be really fun.
Customer	Not sure about walking, but joining a tour might be a good way to travel, because then I might make some friends my own age.

Pause

Agent	Now, let's get some details. Can I have your name, please.
Customer	Yes, it's Su Ming Lee, but you can call me Sue.
Agent	OK, Sue. And what's your address here in Melbourne?
Customer	I'm living with my aunt in the suburb of Kew. It's 29 Loch Street. That's L O C H not L O C K.
Agent	Do you have a phone number that I can get you on?
Customer	The best thing would be if I give you my mobile. I always have it on me. It's 0 4 0 2 double 5 8 double 9 2.
Agent	OK. And when do you want to travel? Because you'll need to be down south in July or August.
Customer	Oh, yes. Of course. That's winter, isn't it? So I'd better go to Auckland in May…

Agent	Yes. Let's say departing from Melbourne on the first of May – that's a Saturday – and then you could begin your course on Monday the third.
Customer	That sounds great!
Agent	And how long would you like to study for? A month, two, three? What do you think?
Customer	Well, I'll probably need more than a month. What about eight weeks… until the end of June.
Agent	Fine. I'll see what I can do. Oh, and how would you like to pay for this?
Customer	On my Visa card if that's possible.

Pause

Agent	Hello Sue. It's Angelo from Kosmos Travel here. I've booked your flight and I've found you an English college called The Harbour Language Centre.
Customer	Great! Where exactly is that?
Agent	Well, have you got that little map I gave you yesterday?
Customer	Yes.
Agent	You see where the harbour is, with the three wharves and the water?
Customer	Yes, got that.
Agent	OK, there are two parallel streets – Quay Street, that's Q U A Y and Customs Street. The building where the college is located is on Quay Street, opposite Princes Wharf.
Customer	Right, got it. And what about accommodation?
Agent	Well, I've booked you into a hotel for the first three nights and then the accommodation officer will find you a family to live with.
Customer	Good. And where's the hotel?
Agent	It's a short walk from the college, on the corner of Queen Street and City Road.
Customer	Which corner exactly?
Agent	On the left-hand side as we are looking at the map.
Customer	OK. Near the little park.
Agent	Yes, that's right.
Customer	And what about a good bookshop? I'm going to need to buy a dictionary and some English books.
Agent	Yes. Well, I believe there's a really good language bookshop on the corner of Customs Street and Queen Street. It's near the college so that's pretty convenient.
Customer	Thank you so much. You've been really helpful.

Section 2 (CD Track 13)

Announcer

The Sydney Harbour Bridge is nearly three-quarters of a century old and, to help celebrate this important occasion, our reporter Sarah Chambers has compiled this brief history of her favourite bridge.

Sarah

A bridge is more than just a crossing over a river or a waterway – it is a landmark in its own right; a landmark which allows us to identify one city from another. Think, for instance, of the Bridge of Sighs in Venice, or the magnificent Charles Bridge in Prague. Each of these cities can be recognised by their famous bridges. The Golden Gate Bridge in San Francisco is another example of a city known by its bridge. But in addition to this, a bridge is a kind of ornament for a city, similar, if you like, to a cathedral or a palace.

Here in Sydney we may not have our own palace, but we do have our famous and much loved bridge – The Sydney Harbour Bridge, which is sometimes affectionately known as 'the coat hanger' because of its arched shape. It was built back in the 1930s, and so the bridge is coming up for a significant birthday. Let's have a little look at its history.

Pause

Although the idea of building a crossing over Sydney harbour had been discussed many years earlier, it wasn't until the year 1916 that the state government agreed to allocate some money for the construction of a bridge.

The chief engineer for the bridge was a man called Dr John Bradfield, a brilliant engineer who supervised the entire project from beginning to end. First they had to decide on a design, so he organised an international competition to choose a design, and ultimately got the one he wanted. The job went to a British engineering firm and the contract was signed in 1924. The design he chose was the single-arch bridge that you see today, made of steel, with a tower at either end.

In 1926, construction finally began. The first thing they had to do was demolish 800 houses around the site where the towers were to be built. The poor families, however, never received any compensation for this! But the project created thousands of jobs – much needed in those difficult times. Of course, like all projects of this size, it took much longer to build than originally planned – it was supposed to have been finished by 1930 – but actually it wasn't completed for another two years. It also cost twice as much as the original quote, coming in at £9.5 million instead of the agreed contract price of £4.2 million! But what's new?

The opening ceremony took place on 19 March 1932, and a large crowd gathered for the occasion. The Premier of the State was just about to cut the ribbon when suddenly a man rode through the crowd mounted on a horse and slashed the ribbon with his sword. He wanted to be the first to cut the ribbon. Anyway, they tied the ribbon back together and the ceremony continued. The man on the horse was fined £5 for his offensive behaviour!

Since then, millions of cars have crossed the bridge, each paying a toll to do so. By the early 1980s the government had paid off the loan for the money they'd borrowed all those years before, but motorists continued to pay to cross from north to south. This money was subsequently used to build a tunnel under the harbour to reduce the amount of traffic on the bridge.

Pause

The tunnel was opened in 1992 and cost $544 million. It is 2·3 kilometres long and is equipped with all the latest technology, including closed circuit television to monitor any problems. And it has most definitely reduced the load on the bridge, as it carries around 75,000 vehicles each day which would otherwise have to use the bridge. And it's apparently strong enough to withstand the impact of a ship or even the impact of an earthquake.

The tunnel has been a welcome solution to Sydney's traffic problems, but, of course, a tunnel could never compete with a bridge as a landmark for any city. So let's wish the bridge a very happy birthday!

Section 3 (CD Track 14)

Mia	Hello, David.
David	Oh hi, Mia. Sorry I'm a bit late.
Mia	Oh. No problem! Thanks for agreeing to help me with my assignment today. I really needed to go over it with someone.
David	Sure. You were going to talk about European rock art, weren't you?
Mia	Yes, the rock drawings in the caves of Lascaux in western France.
David	Oh, fantastic, over 13,000 years old, I believe. What sort of drawings are they?
Mia	They're drawings of animals on the whole, but you can also find some human representations, as well as some signs. There are roughly 600 drawings at Lascaux.
David	Really? Were they mostly pictures of bulls?
Mia	Well, no, actually, the animal most depicted was the horse. Have a look at this graph. It shows the distribution of the different animals. You see… first the horse, and then after that a sort of prehistoric bull…
David	Oh, OK. That's interesting, isn't it?
Mia	…and the third most commonly drawn creature was the stag. There were some other animals but these are the main ones.
David	What are the drawings like? I mean, what sort of style?
Mia	Well, the bulls are depicted very figuratively – they're not very realistic. They are very big by comparison to the other drawings, of people and signs. They appear to be almost three-dimensional in some cases, following the contours of the cave walls, but of course they're not.
David	Amazing. Perhaps they felt these animals were the most impressive and needed to be represented like that.
Mia	Yeah, maybe. The drawings of humans by contrast consist of just simple lines. Like the stick figures my little sister draws. Perhaps humans were seen as less important.
David	Mmm, perhaps. What about the signs. How did they draw them?
Mia	There doesn't appear to be much evidence of signs, and those that have been found are usually made up of little points.
David	Rather like Aboriginal art from Australia.
Mia	Yes. Something like that, but not as complex, of course.
David	So apart from the bulls and horses and stags, were there any other creatures depicted?
Mia	In one or two chambers, you do find pictures of fish but they're quite rare.

Pause

David	What sort of size is the cave? It must be quite large to have that many pictures.
Mia	Well, it's actually a number of inter-linking chambers, really. Here's a map showing where the different drawings can be found.
David	Oh, good. Let's have a look at that.
Mia	The first 20 metres inside the cave slope down very steeply to the first hall in the network. That's called the Great Hall of the Bulls.
David	Here. OK.
Mia	Then off to the left we have the Painted Gallery, which is about 30 metres long, and is basically a continuation of this first hall.
David	But further into the cave.
Mia	Exactly. Then we find a second, lower gallery called the Lateral Passage. This opens off the aisle to the right of the Great Hall of the Bulls. It connects the next chamber with an area known as the Main Gallery. At the end of the Main Gallery is the Chamber of Felines. There are one or two other connecting chambers but there's no evidence of man having been in these rooms.
Pause	
David	Is the cave open to the public today?
Mia	Well, no. Because after the initial discovery in 1940, it was opened and literally millions of people came through to see the drawings. Then in the fifties the experts started to worry about the damage being done to the drawings, and the government finally closed the Lascaux cave in 1963.
David	Is that so!
Mia	It wasn't really the tourists that were doing the harm, but the fact that after thousands of years, the cave was suddenly open to the atmosphere and so bacteria and fungi started to destroy the pictures. You need a special permit to enter the cave now and very few people can get that unless they're scientists or have some official status.
David	It's a shame, but I can see that they had to do something to protect the cave. So that means you can no longer see this rock art.
Mia	Well, not exactly. What they've done is re-create the drawings in a man-made cave, which you can visit.
David	Oh brilliant!
Mia	Yeah, the authorities decided to reproduce the two best sections of the site so they've created a life-size copy of the Hall of the Bulls and of the Painted Gallery. It's just a cement shell, which corresponds in shape to the interior of the original.
David	So now you can visit the caves without actually harming any of the 13,000-year-old paintings.

Section 4 (CD Track 15)

Last week we looked at some general principles associated with marketing and today I'd like to look at some of those points in a little more detail.

So what is marketing? Or put another way, what does the term 'marketing' mean? Many people think of it simply as the process of selling and advertising. And this is hardly surprising when every day we are bombarded with television adverts, mail shots, and telephone sales. But selling and advertising are only two functions of marketing.

In fact, marketing, more than any other business function, deals with customers. So perhaps the simplest definition is this one: marketing is the delivery of customer value and satisfaction at a profit. In other words, finding customers, keeping those customers happy and making money out of the process!

The most basic concept underlying marketing is the concept of human needs. These include basic physical needs for things like food, as well as warmth and safety. And marketers don't invent these needs; they're a basic part of our human make-up. So besides physical needs, there are also social needs – for instance, the need to belong and to be wanted. And in addition to social needs, we have the need for knowledge and self-expression, often referred to as individual needs.

As societies evolve, members of that society start to see things not so much in terms of what they need, but in terms of what they want, and when people have enough money these wants become demands.

Now, it's important for the managers in a company to understand what their customers want if they are going to create effective marketing strategies, so there are various ways of doing this. One way at supermarkets, for instance, is to interview customers while they're doing their shopping. They can be asked about their buying preferences and then the results of the survey can be analysed. This provides reliable feedback on which to base future marketing strategies. It's also quite normal for top executives from department stores to spend a day or two each month visiting stores and mixing freely with the public, as if they were ordinary customers, to get an idea of customer behaviour.

Another way to get information from customers is to give them something. For instance, some fast-food outlets give away vouchers in magazines or on the street that entitle customers to get part of their meal for nothing. As well as being a good way of attracting customers into the restaurants to spend their money, it also allows the managers to get a feel for where to advertise and which age-groups to target.

Another strategy employed at some well-known theme parks such as Disneyland is for top managers to spend at least one day in their career, touring the park dressed as Mickey Mouse or some other cartoon character. This provides them with the perfect opportunity to survey the scene and watch the customers without being noticed.

OK, well we mentioned customer satisfaction at the beginning of this lecture, and I'd like to return briefly to that, as it relates to what we've just been talking about. If the performance of a product falls short of the customer's expectations, the buyer is going to be dissatisfied. In other words, if the product you buy isn't as good as you'd expected, then the chances are you'll be unhappy about it. If, on the other hand, performance matches expectations, and the product you buy is as good as you expected, then generally speaking the buyer is satisfied. But smart companies should aim one step higher. They should aim to delight customers by promising only what they can be sure of delivering, and then delivering much more than they promised. So then, if as sometimes happens, performance is better than expected, the buyer is delighted and is twice as likely to come back to the store.

Now let's move on to look at the role of advertising…

Sample Answer Sheets

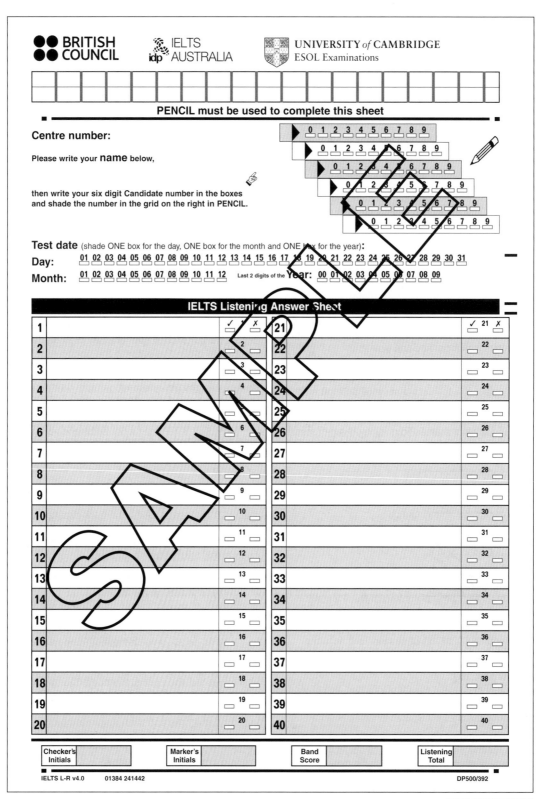

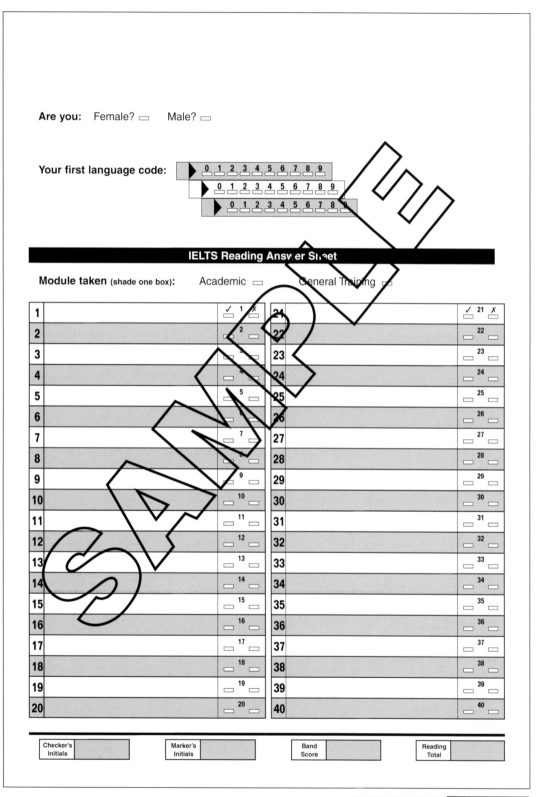

Acknowledgements

The authors and publishers would like to thank the teachers who commented on the material:

Australia: Garry Adams, Peter Gray; Brunei: Caroline Brandt; China: Gang He, Tao Sun, Chenggang Zhou; Japan: Alex Case; New Zealand: Belinda Hayes; Singapore: Jackie Williams; Spain: Chris Turner; Taiwan: Daniel Sansoni; UK: Frances Hughes, Diane Reeves, Karen Saxby, Roger Scott, Clare West, Norman Whitby.

The authors and publishers are grateful to the following for permission to use copyright material in *Action Plan for IELTS*. While every effort has been made, it has not been possible to identify the sources of all the material used and in such cases the publishers would welcome information from the copyright owners:

p. 24: illustration 'Prototype for a plastic car' and for the adapted text for the listening extract 2 (CD track 7) by Daniel Dasey and Colin Hamilton. Copyright © *The Sun-Herald*, August 2004; p. 35: extract 'Power-packed fliers' by Paul Marks, *New Scientist* June 2000 and pp. 99-100: extract 'Sticking power', *New Scientist* December 2000; p. 37: extract 'Sahara' from *Into Harmony with the Planet* by Michael Allaby (Copyright © Michael Allaby 1990), by permission of PFD (www.pfd.co.uk) on behalf of Professor Michael Allaby; p. 38: illustration 'Zinacantan' from *Living World Geography* by Parker & Parker © 1994. By permission of Macmillan Education, Australia; pp. 39 and 40: extract 'The four-minute mile' from Greatest Event in World Sport by Simon Hollingsworth, published in *The Australian* May 2004. Reproduced by permission of Simon Hollingsworth; p. 43: extract 'Effective advertising' from *The Advertising Handbook, 2nd edition* by Sean Brierley © 2002 Routledge; p. 44: extract 'Dawn of Modern Man' from *Focus Magazine* July 2004 and p. 51: extract 'The old library of Alexandria' by Sally Palmer from *Focus Magazine* May 2002; p. 46: extract 'Waste disposal' from *The Economist* August 2004, p. 53: extract 'Gold bugs' from *The Economist* July 2001; p. 57: extract 'Business Bubbles' from *The Economist* October 2002; pp. 102-103: extract 'Try it and see' from *The Economist* March 2002 © The Economist Newspaper Limited; p.48: extract 'Blowing in the wind' from '21st Century Power' supplement, *BBC Wildlife Magazine* September 2002 and p. 75: extract 'On the move' from '21st Century Power' supplement, *BBC Wildlife Magazine* September 2002 © BBC Wildlife Magazine. Reproduced by permission of Origin Publishing; p. 62: diagram from *Oxford Children's Encyclopedia* © Oxford University Press 2004 and p. 104: adapted diagram from *The Oxford Children's A-Z of Technology* by Robin Kerrod © Oxford University Press 1996. Reprinted by permission of Oxford University Press; p 65: chart 'Average nutrient intake' taken from the website www.abs.gov.au. ABS data used with permission of the Australian Bureau of Statistics; p. 68: diagram 'Garden waterfall' from *Reader's Digest Practical Guide to Home Landscaping*. Copyright © Reader's Digest 1990. Reproduced by permission of Reader's Digest (Australia) Pty Limited; pp. 96-97: extract 'Egyptian Architecture' and p. 98: diagram 'Section through pyramid' from *Handbook of Art* by Graham Hopwood. Copyright © Science Press 2003. Reproduced by permission of Science Press.

The publishers are grateful to the following for permission to reproduce copyright photographs and material:

p. 6 (top): Andrew Bannister Gallo Images/CORBIS; pp. 6 (bottom), 30, 58, 78, 80, 84, 88: Paul Mulcahy; p. 16: www.fotoflite.com

Photo research by Val Mulcahy.

The recordings which accompany this book were made at Studio AVP, London.